# TEACHING TEST-TAKING SKILLS

## Helping Students Show What They Know

### Thomas E. Scruggs
### Margo A. Mastropieri

PURDUE UNIVERSITY

Brookline
Books

*A volume in the series on Cognitive Strategy Instruction*
*Series Editor: Michael Pressley*

Copyright © 1992 by Brookline Books

Reprinted, 1995.

**Library of Congress Cataloging-in-Publication Data**

Scruggs, Thomas E., 1948 -
    Teaching test-taking skills: helping students show what they know
/Thomas E. Scruggs, Margo A. Mastropieri.
     p.    cm.
    Includes bibliographical references and index
    ISBN 0-914797-76-X
    1. Test-taking skills. 2. Study, Method of. I. Mastropieri,
Margo A., 1951 -   . II Title.
LB3060.57.S36 1992
371.3'02812 — dc20                           92-4586
                                                                     CIP

*THIS BOOK IS DEDICATED
TO THE MEMORY OF EDWARD B. SCRUGGS.*

# Table of Contents

# Preface

The purpose of this book is to help children become better test-takers. Although we wrote the book for teachers, who have the most direct contact with tests and test administration, we think this book would also be very helpful for parents, many of whom feel their children's test scores do not completely represent their knowledge or ability. Parents may flnd themselves in a unique position to teach their children these strategies because they may have particular insight into what their children do know and they may be able to find the time to practice these skills with their child individually.

If you do wish to develop these skills in your own children, however, please remember that the best test-taking skills training directly reflects the specific formats of the tests being used. Meet with your child's teacher and find out what kind of tests are most likely to be used. Be certain to assure your child's teacher that you simply wish that your child understand the format demands and other requirements of tests as well as possible so that the test score will be the best reflection of his or her abilities. Talk with your child's teacher about these test-taking skills and ask for feedback on your child's test performance. The best way to help your child succeed in school is to form a cooperative working relationship with your child's teachers. This is also a great way to improve their test-taking skills, and help them "show what they know."

We also thank the many students and teachers who have assisted us with our research projects. We specifically thank Janet H. Scruggs and Frances and Dorothy Mastropieri for their continual support.

Thomas Scruggs
Margo Mastropieri

# CHAPTER 1

# Why Teach Test-Taking Skills?

We began conducting research on test-taking skills in 1983. Nearly a decade and 14 research studies later, involving over 1,000 difficult-to-teach students, we have become firm believers in the importance of good test-taking skills in promoting school success. During this same time, we have made numerous presentations of our findings to schools and professional organizations. We have discovered an enormous amount of interest on the part of parents, teachers, and administrators, who generally shared our view that many students are poorly prepared for test-taking situations, and this lack of "test-wiseness" is often responsible for test scores which do not accurately reflect the students' knowledge. In response to those interested individuals, we have written this book.

## FREQUENTLY ASKED QUESTIONS

We begin this book with an overview of test-taking skills, explained within the framework of questions we are most frequently asked. We hope these questions and answers will encourage you to read on in the book to learn how you can help your students show what they know on tests.

### 1. What are test-taking skills?

Millman, Bishop, and Ebel (1965) defined "test-wiseness" as "a subject's capacity to utilize the characteristics and formats of the test and/or the test-taking situation to receive a high score" (p. 707). In other words, students high in "test-wiseness" can score higher than students of equal ability but lacking test-wiseness, by using their knowledge of specific test formats and testing situations to maximize their performance. Test-taking skills, then, are the skills that, when used effectively, contribute to a "test-wise" individual. Although test-wiseness is not completely independent of other cognitive abilities, such as general intelligence (Scruggs & Lifson, 1985), it nonetheless has been demonstrated to have some of its own unique properties (Diamond & Evans, 1972).

Millman and his colleagues made a distinction between test-wiseness and phenomena such as confidence, anxiety, and motivation of the test-taker (we will be addressing these components of good test-taking performance in the third chapter). They developed a taxonomy of test-taking skills, in which they identified six major elements: four of these were considered to be independent of the test maker or test purpose and can be applied to tests generally. Two were considered to be dependent on specific knowledge of the test maker (e.g., the teacher) or test purpose. The four independent elements included:

*(1) Time-using strategies.* Working quickly and efficiently, solving the problems and answering items you know, and saving more difficult items for last.

*(2) Error avoidance strategies.* Paying careful attention to directions, careful marking of answers, and checking answers.

*(3) Guessing strategies.* Making effective use of guessing when it is likely to benefit the test-taker.

*(4) Deductive reasoning strategies.* Applying a variety of

strategies, including eliminating options known to be incorrect, or using content information from the stem (question) or other test information.

The two elements said to be dependent on the test constructor or test purpose include (5) *intent consideration strategies,* which include consideration of the purpose of the test or intent of the test constructor when selecting answers; and (6) *cue using strategies,* which include use of known idiosyncracies of the test maker, such as avoidance of options using words such as "always," "all" or "never" (specific determiners), when it is known that such options are rarely correct. We will be considering these aspects of test-taking in the chapters that follow.

### 2. How do you teach test-taking skills?

How test-taking skills are taught depends on the specific skill or set of skills to be learned, as well as the age and ability of the students. Generally we have taught test-taking skills as classroom lessons, provided direct teaching of the skills in question followed by guided and independent practice on a variety of practice tests with review, and evaluation and feedback of student progress. We feel that teachers should al*ways* consider how students will be required to respond on tests, and be sure they will be able to answer the questions to the best of their ability. Students should practice studying and responding in the way in which their knowledge will later be evaluated. That is, if students will be required to write out essay responses, they should be given opportunities to study and practice writing essay-type responses. During these practice sessions, teachers can determine which, if any, performance deficits are due to inadequate content knowledge, and which are due to inadequate test-taking skills. Applying information learned in one context to another context is a major problem, especially for students having difficulty learning — who are also those most likely to benefit from test-taking skills training.

### 3. What is the difference between teaching test-taking skills and 'teaching to the test'?

We have always made a very strong distinction between teaching *test-taking skills* and *teaching to the test* (Scruggs & Mastropieri, 1988). The aim of test-taking skills training is to improve the overall *validity* of the test by making scores more accurately reflect what students really know. This is done by making sure that students lose points *only* because they do not know the information, and not for some reason unrelated to content knowledge, such as marking an answer choice incorrectly, or misinterpreting the test directions. *Teaching to the test*, on the other hand, refers to directly teaching specific items which will appear on the test. If the entire content being taught is being tested, as in the 100 addition facts, or a weekly spelling list, it makes sense to teach to the test. However, if the items on the test represent only a *sample*, rather than the entire body of information which is expected to have been learned, such as in an IQ test or annual achievement tests, then teaching to the test is clearly inappropriate. In such cases, higher student performance is not associated with a more valid test score, because the knowledge shown on the test is not representative of the level of knowledge of the entire domain of content. Test scores have been raised, but these scores are meaningless as indicators of content knowledge.

*Test-taking skills training* involves teaching directly to the *format* or *other conditions of testing*. It does not involve the teaching of specific items which will appear on the test. For example, students are given practice at using separate answer sheets, filling in the "bubbles" on those answer sheets, locating and keeping their place, and other format-related skills that are discussed in detail in this book. They are not taught specific content likely to be asked on the test.

**4. If students have poor test scores due to poor test-taking skills, isn't that still a good indicator of their poor school performance?**

Many of the skills referred to as test-taking skills, such as using time wisely, carefully thinking before answering, etc., are also important school tasks, but these skills are not being directly tested and evaluated. The title of the test is almost always oriented toward content, such as "Reading Comprehension," or "Civil War," or "Spelling." In such cases, test performance should reflect specific knowledge and ability in these areas.

If teachers or schools wish to have information on "following directions," or "thinking carefully," they should directly test these areas.

In many cases, students characterized as "special" or "remedial" exhibit difficulties transferring learned information to a different context. When such transfer failures occur, it is important for teachers to distinguish whether these failures reflect low levels of knowledge, or inadequate skill in applying learned information to new situations. Such information is gained when the purposes of tests are clearly specified, and content knowledge is not confused with application knowledge.

**5. Aren't these test-taking skills just tricks to inflate test scores and make teachers look better?**

Absolutely not! In our opinion, training of test-taking skills can help make better teachers! Many teachers have commented how frustrating it is that information students have been taught, and have learned, is not answered correctly on tests. In part, this is because the information has been incompletely taught. In our book, *Effective Instruction for Special Education* (Mastropieri &

Scruggs, 1987), we argue that information is learned through several stages: initial acquisition, fluency, application, and generalization. According to this model, students can have acquired information, and even become fluent at it, and yet fail when they have to apply the information appropriately or generalize that information to a novel test-taking situation. For example, we have frequently encountered teachers who have had students practice their spelling words by *identifying* correct spellings of these words, but then assess students' performance by *producing* or writing the correct spelling. In these cases, students may have performed better if the teachers had the students practice in the same format in which they will be tested. What we are teaching in this book, then, is not a set of 'tricks,' but a method for teaching which includes procedures for applying newly learned content in test-taking situations students encounter.

### 6. Which students need to be taught test-taking skills?

We have rarely encountered a student who had little or nothing to gain from training in test-taking skills. Some students have better test-taking skills than others. How much (or little) students know about test-taking skills can be assessed using procedures described in the next chapter. We have found that younger students, students of all ages characterized as "special" or "remedial," or culturally diverse students, and students from lower socio-economic backgrounds, may benefit particularly from test-taking skills training (Diamond, Ayrer, Fishman, & Green, 1976; Dillard, Warrior-Benjamin, & Perrin, 1977; Dreisbach & Keogh, 1982; Kalechstein, Kalechstein, & Doctor, 1981; McPhail, 1978; Oakland, 1972; Scruggs, White, & Bennion, 1986; Scruggs & Lifson, 1985; Scruggs & Mastropieri, 1988). It is also true that many of these students, often functioning at the edge of academic competence, have the most to gain from such training.

*7. How much improvement can you expect from test-taking skills training?*

The expected level of improvement depends on many factors, including the functioning level of the students, the extent to which test-taking skills are already being used, the length, adequacy, and intensity of the training, and the degree of complexity of test formats. In our own research on standardized tests, we have found that gains of 10-15 percentile points, or six months of school achievement, are common, and that some individual gains are much greater (e.g., Scruggs & Mastropieri, 1986; Scruggs, Mastropieri, & Veit, 1986; Scruggs & Tolfa, 1985). On teacher-made classroom tests, improvements of one letter grade or more have commonly been reported (e.g., Lee & Alley, 1981). Additional research documenting the effects of training in test-taking skills has been described by Bangert-Drowns, Kulik, and Kulik (1983); Callenbach (1973); Costar (1980); Eakins, Green, and Bushnell (1976); Ford (1973); Fuyeo (1971); Gross (1977); Hughes (1985); Kreit (1968); Ortar (1960); Sarnacki (1979); Scruggs & Marsing (1988); Slakter, Koehler, and Hampton (1970); Stevenson (1976); and Wahlstrom and Boersma (1968). All these authors argue that students frequently do know more than their usual test scores indicate, and score higher after they have been shown how to work on test materials more effectively.

Obviously, no degree of test-taking skills training can replace solid knowledge of relevant academic content. However, a thorough knowledge of test-taking skills, combined with a solid knowledge of content, can do much to make the difference between academic success or failure with many students. In our opinion, as much effort as possible should be made to help students "show what they know!"

# CHAPTER 2

# Assessing Test-Taking Skills

All students are not equal when using test-taking skills effectively. The first step in remedying this problem is to determine what skills your students possess, which they lack, and their level of competence. Once the problems are located, you can use information from this book to train deficient or inefficient skills. If your students are adept in the use of test-taking skills, your major teaching responsibility will be in providing further skill and content instruction.

Test-taking skills have been assessed by researchers and practitioners using a variety of methods. These methods include (1) tests of test-taking skills, (2) "passage independence" tests, (3) direct interviews, (4) use of test formats, and (5) evaluating the results of test-taking skills training. In this chapter, we discuss each approach separately.

## TESTS OF TEST-TAKING SKILLS

Slakter, Koehler, and Hampton (1970) were among the first to develop a test of "test-wiseness". In this test, they developed "real" test items in such areas as mathematics, science and social studies, so that the test appeared genuine. Then, within these items, they placed "test-wiseness" items. These items, made up by the authors, could only be answered correctly by the test-taker who was using a specific test-taking strategy.

## Similar Options

Here is one of the "test-wiseness" items Slakter, Koehler, and Hampton used:

When Bestor crystals are added to water:

    1. Heat is given off;

    2. The temperature rises;

\* 3. The solution turns blue;

    4. The container becomes warmer.

As there is no such thing as "Bestor crystals," the answer can only be answered by a "deductive reasoning" strategy. The correct answer to this question is (3) the solution turns blue. But, how can there be a correct answer to a nonsensical question? Because, the "correct" answer means the student used the optimal test-taking strategy, given the correct answer was not known. In this case, the deductive reasoning strategy of choice is referred to as "similar options." This strategy is appropriate because items (1), (2), and (4) all refer to the temperature increasing. Since these three items cannot all be correct (the directions specified choice of only one item), the correct answer must be (3).

It probably has occurred to you that such items are never found on "real" tests. The reason this item appears so contrived is that it is necessary to be absolutely certain that the answer is unknown to students, who must therefore rely on their test-taking skills to answer the question. The only way to be certain that students do not know the answers is to invent the item. It is also true that such "similar options" choices, in the form presented, rarely if ever appear on "real" tests. This is also true; however, it must be remembered that students almost always have some prior knowledge of the content being tested. Given a certain amount of knowledge of a subject, although incomplete, you can see how students might have enough knowledge of the content to see that two items are stating very similar information, in different ways. If there are four item choices, eliminating those two items automatically doubles the probability (from 25% to 50%) of a correct "guess." In addition, if a third item can be eliminated on the basis of another test-taking strategy, the student can be assured of a correct response. This increase in the probability of obtaining a correct response, given partial, but not complete, information, is one of the main purposes of test-taking skills training.

Other types of deductive reasoning strategies assessed by Slakter and his colleagues are given below:

## Stem Options

Here is an example of a "stem options" item:

2. The hungry coyote in Tippecanoe county was observed:

>         a. sleeping in a ditch;
> *       b. stalking prey;
>         c. looking for shelter;
>         d. near the park;

This strategy makes use of information in the stem (or in the stem of a related test item) in making a choice. In this case, the correct answer is "b", because of the relationship between the adjective "hungry" in the stem, and the logical consequence of hunger in a coyote, stalking prey. Again, as with the "similar options" strategy, such a strategy is useful on a "real" test when partial knowledge of the content reveals an insight from the stem that a student with no content knowledge would not necessarily notice.

## Absurd Options

An example of another type of item, absurd options, is the following:

3.  Eskimos make rope for hunting and gathering from:

   a. cotton fibers from their fields;

* b. strips cut from animal hide;

   c. fibers taken from jungle vines;

   d. from palm tree leaves, woven together.

The "absurd options" strategy is commonly employed by test takers, and involves eliminating items known (by the test taker) to be absurd. This does not mean to imply that it is only useful on tests containing "absurd" items; in this case, partial knowledge of the test taker can render an item absurd which may not seem so to a completely uninformed test taker. In this instance, a test taker who is aware that Eskimos live in very cold regions will realize that options "a", "c", and "d" are not possible, as cotton, jungle vines, and palm trees are not found in snowbound regions. The test-taker possessing this strategy, then, will answer "b" by means of elimination, even though she does not know the specific piece of information.

Remember, the test item does not require that the test-taker have complete and final information on a given subject; all that is required on this type of item is that the test-taker can discriminate among four possibilities, and choose the most appropriate option.

## Specific Determiners

Following is a "specific determiners" example:

4.   Individuals who consume excessive sugar:

        a. always suffer from tooth decay;

        b. never have sufficient energy;

  * c. often gain weight;

        d. never eat food high in fiber or vitamins.

This strategy takes advantage of the fact that things are less likely to be "always" or "never" true than they are to be "sometimes", "often," or "rarely" true. However, it also is not "always" true that answers with "always" or "never" are necessarily false! But, given that test-takers with partial information may be able to think of one single case which can eliminate one or more items from consideration, they will have a higher probability of scoring correctly on the item.

## Validity

Slakter and his colleagues (Crehan, Gross, Koehler, & Slakter, 1978) administered tests with these types of items included within "real" items to a large sample of students, and reported that scores of the "test-wiseness" items improved with the age of the students taking the test. They concluded that this test measured a real ability, and that this ability increased with age, perhaps on account of continued exposure to test-taking experiences.

Scruggs and Marsing (1988) reported that a sample of special education students exhibited lower than average levels of performance on a "test wiseness" test, but that their ability to learn and apply these strategies improved greatly after training. We discuss training techniques later in this book.

## A Test-Taking Skills Test

In the Appendix, we have included a sample of test-taking skills items, many based on those developed by Lois Marsing, which can be embedded within "real" test items to estimate the kind of skills your students have in this area. Write a test which includes real items you think your students can answer. After every few real items, place one of the test-taking skills items, so that students will think there is a true answer. Your test could look something like this:

TEST OF GENERAL KNOWLEDGE

Circle the letter next to the correct answer. There is no penalty for incorrect guessing.

1.   The closest estimate of *pi* is:

a. 4.3

* b. 3.1

c. 1.3

d. 1.4

2.   The diameter of the earth is:

* a. 8,000 miles

b. 10,000 miles

c. 12,000 miles

d. 14,000 miles

3.  The fragile plenophla plant:

> a. can grow in any soil
>
> b. can withstand a wide variety of tempera-
> ture
>
> c. tolerates poor moisture conditions
>
> * d. grows best in very special soil.

4.  The Civil War was fought during the period:

> * a. 1860-1865
>
> b. 1840-1845
>
> c. 1770-1776
>
> d. 1940-1945.

5.  The Western Redthroat:

> a. is a bird
>
> * b. is a type of trout
>
> c. has feathers and flies
>
> d. builds nests and lays eggs.

6.  The railroad engineer Casey Jones:

> a. wrote a popular folk song
>
> b. worked on the transcontinental railroad
>
> c. was a Civil War hero
>
> * d. died in a railroad accident.

Questions number 3 and 5, of course, are "test-taking skills" items taken from the Appendix. You should embed at least four of each type of item (e.g., stem options) in the test. If students miss one or more of any type, they will probably benefit from training on these skills. It may also help to use interview techniques, described later in this chapter, to determine whether they really used the test-taking skill.

# PASSAGE INDEPENDENCE TESTS

Another way of assessing test-taking skills is by administering standardized test items which are intended to refer to an accompanying reading passage, and omitting the passage. Students are given test questions from, for example, "reading comprehension" tests, but are not given the reading passages on which these questions are based. You would think it would be impossible to answer any questions testing comprehension of an unread passage, but it is possible to answer many of these questions using one's existing general knowledge and test-taking skills. A class of undergraduate college students were able to answer over half of such questions, without having read the passages they were supposedly comprehending! (Lifson, Scruggs & Bennion, 1984).

How is it possible to answer questions which refer to non-existent reading passages? First, they may know the content! But second, they may use a "guessing" strategy, in which the test-taker realizes it is almost always better to guess than to leave an answer blank. Many students do not realize this, but the probability of a correct guess (given four response options) is 25%, while the probability of a correct response for an answer left blank is zero! We found that students who reported guessing scored much higher than would be expected by chance, evidence that guesses are often more than "guesses".

In addition to guessing strategies, passage independence tests can also be correctly answered by use of prior knowledge, deductive reasoning ability, elimination of incorrect items, and use of information from previous items. For example, consider the following item:

1.  This passage was mostly about:
    * a. lizards;
    b. the weather;
    c. dogs;
    e. squirrels.

Such a question, by itself, is impossible to answer correctly by anything other than a lucky guess. However, what if the following item were also included in the test:

4.  Which of the following is *not* true of lizards?
    a. they have eyelids;
    b. they are reptiles;
    * c. their lay their eggs in ponds;
    d. they eat insects.

A test taker with some prior knowledge, or ability to use elimination strategies, may be able to correctly answer "c". This item strongly suggests that the correct answer to the previous question (1) is "a". It may seem that such items never appear on standardized reading comprehension tests, but we found very similar items on commonly used standardized tests. On one test, over 25% of the test items could be answered without referring to the accompanying passage!

You can use test items such as these to determine how well your students can employ test-taking skills to answer questions they should not be able to answer. Pass out reading comprehension questions from any relevant classroom materials you have, and ask students to do their best to answer, even though they have not read the passage.

You will probably also find that some of your students are much better at answering than other students, and that many of your students would likely benefit from test-taking skills training. In our own research (Scruggs & Lifson, 1986), we have found that some children, including those characterized as "learning disabled", were seen to be much less efficient than more average students at this type of test. If you discuss the task with your class after they have taken it, you will probably be able to identify who has the best test-taking skills, and begin to think of how these skills can be shared with other students.

As with the test-wiseness tests, students never take passage independence tests of the type described here. However, how students perform on such a test may reflect their ability to cope with adverse conditions on tests with time limits or incomplete content knowledge. As with other tests of test-taking skills, passage independence tests can provide you with important information about the way your students approach tests.

## Direct Interviews

Direct interviewing techniques should be used soon after your students have completed a test, real or not. Students, especially those who usually test poorly, should be questioned individually regarding their reasons for each choice they made. Alternatively, if the students' scores are not important, you can present students with examples of test items and ask them to "think aloud" while they are completing the items. Using interview techniques, you can acquire important information about how your students approach tests, what they are thinking while they are choosing answers, and specific reasons for the test-taking decisions they make.

## Procedures

In our research (Scruggs, Bennion, & Lifson, 1985a, 1985b), we individually interviewed students concerning the choices they had made on standardized test items. We asked students to read passages aloud so we could tell if their errors were due to misreadings. Then, after each answer choice, or a set of answer choices, we asked students to tell us why they had chosen the answer they had. At first, we did not know whether students would simply say they knew the answer or that they did not know the answer. What they told us, however, was that they used a great variety of different strategies or routines for arriving at their answer choice.

We found that the type of strategies they reported using were strongly related to test performance. Poorer test-takers' strategy reports included "I don't know what I did with that one," reported misreading test cues or directions, having skipped the item by mistake, or "guessed." Those with higher test scores reported, "I thought I remembered it in the passage, so I went back and found it," (text referring strategy) or "I thought it must be true because of what it says in this sentence" (inferring strategy). In the middle range were vague reports such as, "I thought it sounded right," which were nonetheless more likely to result in correct responses than were the lower-level reports.

When conducting these interviews, we also found that some students, particularly those characterized as "special education" or "remedial," are much less efficient at employing effective strategies than are other students. This was true even when we accounted for their generally lower level of reading ability, and suggests that, for these students, particular attention should be paid to students' thought processes when taking tests.

When using interviewing strategies, it seems important to conduct them with one student at a time, in a quiet area. Write down students' responses as they are given, and encourage students to say as much as they can about their thinking, even if it makes little sense at first. It is also important to listen to them read the problems and solve them so that you can get an idea of how they function. It is important to know how poor readers approach tests. Do they know when they can ask for help with reading and when they can not? Do they know how to gain the most information from reading the words they do know, or do they give up easily, and make random guesses? Such information will have strong implications for training.

If you can not easily write all the responses as they are given, you could use a tape recorder or video recorder, and transcribe responses later. When evaluating student responses, use the techniques described in this book to determine the level of appropriateness of the strategies they reported.

For example, in reading comprehension tests, students should determine whether questions are recall or inference questions. For recall questions, students should refer back to the passage to be sure their answer is correct. For inference questions, students should realize the answer is not explicitly in the passage, but they should look for something in the passage which would lead them to believe a certain answer is correct. Some students may be more, or less, able to determine whether the test question requires recall or inference on the part of the test taker. When strategy reports are compared with what seem to be optimal strategies, you will have a good idea what type of test-taking skills training you should implement.

Another question we asked students, once they had made an answer choice, was how certain they were the answer was correct. We found many students were very good at predicting the overall accuracy of their answers but many students, including many with learning disabilities, did not predict correctness well, and often overestimated the likelihood that a given answer was correct. The ability to evaluate correctness of one's own response is important for test-taking. If students cannot estimate the correctness of their responses, they will not know whether they should try to correct them.

*Example of interview techniques.* Here is an example of **reading comprehension** test questions:

> Many years ago, Indians of the hot desert built their homes with earth. A very old tribe, called the Ho-Ho-Kam, built the first tall house in America. They made adobe bricks with earth, grass, and water, and built their "big house" with them. They stored grain in the "big house." The "big house" is three stories high and still stands today. It is known by the Spanish name for "big house," Casa Grande.

6.  Adobe bricks are made of:
    - f. pieces of rock
    - g. earth, grass, and water
    - h. sand
    - i. concrete.

7.  In the passage, what is meant by Ho-Ho-Kam?
    - a. a type of adobe brick
    - b. a desert sun
    - c. a very old Indian tribe
    - d. a big house.

Here is some sample dialogue of a teacher interviewing a student on test-taking skills:

Teacher:   Can you read the next paragraph and answer the questions?

Student:   I guess so...[Reads] "Many years ago, Indians of the hot de- desert built their homes with earth. A very old tribe, called the Ho...Ho... — I can't read that — built the first tall house in America. They made abood? — alone? — bricks with earth, grass, and water, and built their "big house" with them. Three stor — storied grain in the "big house." The "big house" is three stories high and still stands today. It is known by the Spanish name for 'big house,' Casa Grand."

Teacher:   Now read the questions.

Student:   [Reads] "6. A-body bricks are made of - " I can't read it.

Teacher:   What answer do you think it is?

Student:   I don't know... f?

Teacher:   Why did you choose "f" for your answer?

Student:   I couldn't read it, so I just guessed the first one....

Teacher:   Do you think you answered that one correctly?

Student:   I think I might have...I'm pretty sure its right.

Teacher:   How about the next one?

Student:   [Reads] "7. In the pass - age, what is meant by Ho - Home?" "a".

Teacher:   Why did you choose "a"?

Student:   I couldn't read that one, either, so I guessed.

This student reported using a guessing strategy, simply because he could not read a few of the words in the passage. He should be taught to identify the appearance of the word, even if he can not read it, and to look back in the passage for the correct answer, "g". In this case, it is simply not necessary to be able to read every word in the passage in order to answer the questions correctly, and the student needs to be made aware of this. But he should have read — or attempted to read — every answer choice, and carefully chosen from among them. He also should realize that such blind guessing, although better than not answering at all, is very unlikely to be correct. More information on the type of test-taking strategies most appropriate for different types of questions is given later in this book. Nevertheless, you can see that the direct interview technique can give you much useful information regarding each student's knowledge of test-taking skills.

# USE OF TEST FORMATS

## Item Format

Test formats can be a particular source of difficulty for some students (Dunn & Goldstein, 1959; Rowley, 1974;

Tolfa, Scruggs, & Bennion, 1985). Sometimes, specific test formats can be used to determine whether students are likely to have difficulty in manipulating these formats. We can describe two examples from our own research regarding how this can be done. In one instance (Scruggs, Bennion, & Lifson, 1985b), we encountered an item type that we predicted might be confusing to our students. It was a reading decoding test, but, since decoding skills can not be assessed directly on group administered pencil-and-paper tests, the items looked something like this:

Choose the answer that sounds most like the under-lined sound:

br<u>ow</u>n

     a. bright

     b. loan

     c. found

Many students may incorrectly choose "a", due to the similarity of the beginnings of the words, even though they were familiar with the pronunciation of "ow" diphthongs. The fact that, for some students, "bright" (or a similar distractor) is the most popular item choice, indicated these students needed additional practice on the format of the test.

## Separate Answer Sheets

In another instance (Veit & Scruggs, 1986), we wanted to know how well our students could use separate answer sheets. Some previous research had suggested that many first and second graders have substantial difficulty with the use of separate answer sheets. We wanted to know whether learning disabled fourth graders would also have difficulty with this format. However, since we did not want knowledge of test content to interfere with use of the answer sheet, we identified each correct answer on the test booklet with an arrow. Students were told to transfer the correct answer from the booklet to the answer sheet. What we found was that some students were far more adept at this skill than others. Some students were able to work very fast and accurately; others could work accurately but at a slower rate; still others were neither fast or particularly accurate. However, few would argue that ability to use a separate answer sheet should be a major component of a reading achievement score! This investigation of format variables demonstrated that some students could clearly benefit from training in use of separate answer sheets.

**TASK: You should test your students' ability to use separate answer sheets so this problem does not obscure what they know.** First, construct a test and accompanying answer sheet that looks just like the tests your students take. Do not include any critical test items. Identify the correct item on the test with an arrow or other mark. We placed the arrow at the end rather than the beginning of the correct item. Our hunch is that students' eyes are probably at the end of the item when they must look for the proper place on the answer sheet. Tell your students to identify the correct item and color it in as quickly as possible on the answer sheet. Place a time limit on the task so it will more closely resemble test conditions.

When students have finished, check their answer sheets for speed, correctness, and correct coloring in of answer choices. Any student who exhibits more than minor problems may benefit from some additional guided practice on the use of separate answer sheets.

## TRAINING TEST-TAKING SKILLS

The final way of assessing test-taking skills is really a way to validate your training of these skills. If your students' test scores increase as a result of training of these test-taking skills in your classroom, you know that those students lacked critical test-taking skills that they now possess! In some of our own training programs, we found that students could gain as much as 10-15 percentile points, or 4-6 months of academic achievement, and yet we did not teach any of the content being tested! (Scruggs & Mastropieri, 1986; Scruggs, Mastropeiri & Veit, 1986; Scruggs & Tolfa, 1985). The students were deficient in test-taking skills, and our programs successfully trained these skills. When you implement a test skills training program, pre-test your students prior to the training, and post-test them at the end. You can show your students how much better they are taking tests, and their worries about taking tests will decrease.

# CHAPTER 3

# General, All-Purpose Test-Taking Skills

In this chapter, we consider strategies that should be helpful to any individual test-taker. Although these are not always referred to as specific test-taking skills, we consider each helpful for students taking virtually any kind of test. We therefore describe them as **all-purpose** strategies, in contrast to the very specific strategies we discuss later, which address very specific test formats. The **all-purpose** strategies include (1) academic preparation strategies, (2) physical preparation strategies, (3) attitude-improving strategies, (4) anxiety reducing strategies, and (5) motivational strategies.

## ACADEMIC PREPARATION

The most important component of good general test-taking skills, of course, is a thorough knowledge of the content being tested. The most important test-taking strategies are of little use to a student who possesses no knowledge of the test content. And this is as it should be. The purpose of test-taking skill training is to enhance the student's ability to show what he knows.

The best way to prepare academically for a test is by studying the content to be tested. Many of the most important strategies are "study skills" rather than test-taking skills. These skills, although very important, are beyond the scope of of this particular book. For information on general "study skills" strategies, consult Carman and Adams (1977). When tests involve recall of specific academic content (and they very frequently do), "mnemonic" (memory-enhancing) strategies can be extremely effective. Use of mnemonic strategies to enhance memory for school content is described in detail in *Teaching Students Ways to Remember: Strategies for Learning Mnemonically*, our other book in this series (Mastropieri & Scruggs, 1991).

There are several academic preparation strategies appropriate for preparing to take tests. In contrast to the study skills and mnemonic strategies just mentioned, academic preparation strategies do not specify *how* students should study, but rather *what* and *when* they should study.

## Test Content

Before starting to study, it is important that students know what content they will be tested on. Students often waste valuable study time by studying content that is unlikely to appear on the test. The teacher should help students determine what is likely to be covered on the test before studying.

The most obvious way for students to learn what content is likely to be on the test is by asking their teacher. While many teachers resent being asked whether very specific information will appear on the test (e.g., "Do we have to know the date of the Treaty of Ghent for the test?"), teachers should define what will be covered on the test, and answer general questions from their students (e.g., "Will we be required on the test to remember specific dates?"). You should recommend general areas for study and identify the materials the student will be responsible for. Giving general information about the test gives away little and helps your students focus on the important knowledge rather than the trivial.

If you are not the content teacher, but are working as

a resource teacher or in some other advisory capacity, teach your student(s) to **effectively question** the content teacher about what content will likely appear on the test. The student should ask such questions in a way which reflects a sincere desire to learn what is important and to do well in the course.

Another way to help students focus on the content most likely to be tested is to give the students a practice test in the same area of study. Explain that the real test will probably cover some similar material, but will not be exactly the same. Since teachers give similar tests throughout the year, students could benefit by seeing what type of questions were on a previous test.

As a resource or consulting teacher, you may be familiar with the type of tests a particular teacher is likely to give, or can get prior tests from the teacher for practice. It is important to help the student learn to distinguish between the general type of information on the coming test which will honestly help the student while studying, and overly specific "insider" information which may put students at an unfair advantage.

## Test Format

Students should know the type of questions that will appear on a test, and teachers should feel comfortable telling them such information, since it will focus their studying efforts. For example, if you plan to ask essay questions, you should prepare students to write about general principles and concepts, and more specifically about the topic(s) on the test. If you plan to use multiple choice questions, students should be aware that they will be required simply to identify, rather than generate, information. Although identification formats are generally less difficult than producing information, multiple choice tests often focus on the identification of a large amount of less important information. These different formats have very different implications for studying, and students should be made aware before the test occurs.

If students are not told the structure and focus of he upcoming test, they should ask their teacher(s). If they cannot get the information, have students consider the type of tests which the teacher has administered in the past. If the students cannot determine for certain which formats are likely, they should prepare so they are ready for any format they may encounter. We provide information on how to address these different types of test formats later in this book.

## Planning for Tests

The most efficient way for students to prepare for a test involves studying for the test as new content is introduced, and the teacher lectures are still fresh. Misunderstandings about course content should be clarified as they arise; students should not wait until the day before an exam to discover they do not understand important content. Teachers should give "practice tests," so the students can practice producing the information in a situation similar to the actual test situation. Level of performance obtained on these "practice tests" can be used as important predictors of actual test performance. It can help the student see the kinds of problems he or she needs to address when taking the test.

# PHYSICAL PREPARATION

When taking a test, it is important that your students be prepared physically as well as mentally. This is best accomplished by encouraging them to establish healthy patterns of eating and sleeping prior to the test situation. Long hours of "cramming" the night before a test are of little use if the test-taker has sacrificed mental alertness at the time of the test. Students should be strongly encouraged to study early in the semester and early in the day, when minds are fresher, and time for a good night's sleep can be allowed. In some cases, it may be helpful for students to go to bed *early* on the night before a test, to assure proper sleep, and arise early, to study and review one last time on the day of the test. Early morning studying is often far more productive than late night studying, when mind and body are tired, and the student must fight off sleep as well as concentrate on the subject matter.

It is important for teachers to encourage their students to eat properly before taking a test. Students who have not had an adequate breakfast can be expected to encounter an energy slump, particularly late in the morning. Students who have eaten breakfast but skipped lunch can also expect to slump later in the afternoon. Although many students, particularly at secondary age levels, control their own eating, it is important to make them aware that proper nutrition, especially on the day of the test, can help them answer the questions more alertly, and so improve their test scores.

Finally, overall physical fitness also plays a role in test-taking success, as it does in virtually all areas of school functioning. Unlike eating and sleeping patterns, however, physical fitness and stamina can not be addressed especially on test days. Students must keep fit throughout the academic year. Regular exercise, conducted properly, can greatly increase energy levels that lead to increased achievement in many different areas of school functioning.

# IMPROVING ATTITUDES

When taking any test, students should maintain a positive, confident attitude. Attitudes conducive to good test-taking are not fatalistic ("I'll never pass") or apathetic ("who cares how I do?"); nor are they overly optimistic ("I can get an 'A' without even trying"). Rather, appropriate test attitudes are positive and confident but tempered with caution: "I can do well on this test if I stay alert and try my best."

## Evaluating Attitudes

How can you evaluate your students' attitudes toward tests? In our own research (Scruggs, Mastropieri, Tolfa, & Jenkins, 1985; Tolfa, Scruggs, & Mastropieri, 1985), we developed a 10-item, easily administered survey that proved to be highly reliable. It contained the following items:

Attitude Toward Tests Survey

Circle YES or NO

YES  NO  1. Taking a test is my favorite thing to do at school.

YES  NO  2. Sometimes I am nervous when I take a test.

YES  NO  3. I look forward to taking a test.

YES  NO  4. I dislike taking a test when I don't know the answers.

YES  NO  5. I wish we had fewer tests.

YES  NO  6. Taking a test is always fun.

YES  NO  7. I like tests even when I don't know the answers.

YES  NO  8. Taking a test is one of the worst things about school.

YES  NO  9. I would rather do something else besides take a test.

YES  NO  10. I wish we had more tests.

Normally achieving elementary aged students taking this type of survey answered about 60% of the items positively on average (either "yes" to a positively worded item or "no" to a negatively worded item). About 2/3 of the students answered from 3 to 8 items positively. Neither excessively negative nor excessively positive attitudes seemed appropriate. For example, it would seem reasonable to answer "yes" to Item #2 ("Sometimes I am nervous when I take a test"); however, an answer of "yes" to Item #1 ("Taking a test is my favorite thing to do at school") may be inappropriately positive.

We also found that, after taking an achievement test, student attitudes on this survey became more extreme. More students make either very positive or very negative choices. After training in test-taking skills, however, students did not exhibit these extreme attitudes, probably because they knew what was expected of them and were able to be more realistic in their approach to the test. Appropriately positive attitudes toward tests, rather than unqualified enthusiasm or pessimism, are most desirable.

If you administer this survey to your own students, score 1 point for each "yes" answer on items 1, 3, 6, 7, and 10; score 1 point for each "no" answer on items 2, 4, 5, 8, and 9. Students who score less than three, or more than eight, may not have arealistic attitude toward taking a test.

## How to Improve Attitudes

If you have reason to believe that some students have an inappropriate attitude toward taking tests, consider the following recommendations:

1. Are students' *standards* for themselves too high? Perhaps they would benefit from a calm discussion about what they can reasonably expect from themselves. If they set reasonable goals for themselves, yet continue to strive for improvement, they may find their attitude improving.

2. Do students get *frustrated* easily? One source of problems with tests is that tests may contain items that only a very small proportion of students are expected to answer correctly, or that students of different age groups are expected to score differently on. If students are informed they are often not expected to answer all test items correctly, they may begin to consider test-taking a less punishing experience.

3. Are they afraid of being *evaluated negatively*? You should develop and maintain an environment that expects and rewards effort and efficiency. Students should feel that if they have tried their best, and not wasted time or resources, that you will be pleased with them. Make certain that your words and deeds communicate your true expectation that students try their best, and that if they do, you will regard them positively — and that their peers should do likewise.

4. Are they uncertain of *what to expect* on tests? Give them experience with short practice tests, similar in format to the tests they will encounter.

5. Are they uncertain about *how to best approach* a test? Teach them the "test-taking skills" described in this book! We have found that test taking skills training has resulted in better attitudes towards testing (Scruggs, 1985).

6. Do they experience *test anxiety*? In that case, use the anxiety-reducing strategies described in the next section.

# REDUCING
# ANXIETY

A limited amount of anxiety, properly channeled, can actually help students maintain their alertness while taking a test (Meichenbaum & Butler, 1980); however, excessive levels of anxiety can inhibit students' clear thinking and hinder their performance on a test (Wine, 1980). Appropriate training can have a positive effect on reducing anxiety levels and increasing appropriate attention to the task (Phi Delta Kappa, 1989; Schwarzer, van der Ploeg, & Spielberger, 1982; 1983; Sarason, 1980b).

Anxiety connected with taking tests has commonly been measured by the Test Anxiety Scale for Children (Sarason, 1978; 1980a). Overall, children who score high on the anxiety scale have been shown to score lower on achievement tests than low-anxious students. Low-achieving students tend to get even lower test scores as a result of anxiety (Sarason, 1980b).

Anxiety can inhibit test performance because it causes the test-taker to focus on "off task" thoughts during the testing situation. Test-anxious students tend to report thinking about being evaluated negatively, imagining the consequences of performing poorly, wondering how other students are doing, thinking fruitlessly and too long about alternate answers, or characterizing themselves as inadequate (Meichenbaum & Butler, 1980; Sarason, 1980b). When students are thinking such worrisome thoughts, they cannot be thinking clearly about test information, and therefore are more likely to "blank out" when trying to retrieve important information.

There are several strategies you can employ to help your students reduce their anxiety during test situations (Allen, Elias, & Zlotlow, 1980; Denney, 1980; Erwin & Dinwiddie, 1980). These strategies are described below.

## Experience with Test Formats and Test-Taking Skills

Students are likely to be less anxious about things that are familiar to them. They are also likely to be less anxious when they have been taught how to respond to anxiety-provoking stimuli. For these reasons, giving your students prior exposure to tests and teaching test-taking skills, as described in detail in following chapters, is likely to be very helpful in reducing test-related anxiety.

## Teacher Comments

Test-anxious students have been seen to perform better when teachers make fewer evaluative comments during test administration. Comments you may make to your students about the possible negative consequences of poor test performance, or comments about the necessity for a "top" score may not be helpful to anxious students. Anxious students may actually perform better when you remind them that they are not expected to answer all questions correctly, and that in some cases, they may not finish all test items; but, if they work carefully and cautiously, they will have done a good job. Here are some examples of teacher comments that may be helpful, and teacher comments that may not be helpful:

### Comments That May Be Related to Test Anxiety

*Helpful comments:* "You should be proud of how hard you have worked this semester."

"If you try hard, and use all the test-taking skills we have practiced, I'm sure I'll be proud of your work."

"When you take this, just think about the test, not about

anything else. Your score isn't anybody else's business."

*Not helpful comments:* "You'll need an 'A' on this test just to pass the course."

"This test is easy. Everybody should get a 'hundred' on it."

"I'll post the scores on the bulletin board so everybody can see how they did."

## Self-Monitoring

*On-task thinking.* Anxious thoughts contribute to lower levels of concentration on test content, and lower the probability of answering correctly. Teach anxious students to monitor their thoughts, to detect when their thinking is cognitively "on-task" or "off-task," and how to initiate "on-task" thinking when necessary. Teach students to discriminate between *on-task* and *off-task* thinking. Examples of on-task thinking: specific thoughts regarding problem solutions, checking work, or checking how much time is left. Examples of off-task thinking: wondering what score will be obtained, wondering about the examiners' opinion of the test-taker, thinking about negative consequences of poor performance, and wondering how other students are performing. As practice, students should periodically (a timer may be helpful at first), ask themselves what they are thinking, write down the thought, evaluate the thought (on- or off-task), and say or write an on-task thought when necessary. In some cases a self-monitoring sheet, in which students check, at intervals, whether their thoughts were on-task or off-task, will be beneficial. Here is an example:

SELF-MONITORING SHEET
On-Task Thinking

This sheet will help you monitor your thoughts during a test. Each time the timer rings, check whether your thoughts were "on-task" or "off-task." Here are some examples:

*Off-task thinking:* "I can't do this." "What will my teacher think?" "I wonder if everybody else is ahead of me." "I wonder how the other kids answered this question." "What will happen if I don't do well on this?"

*On-task thinking:* "What do I need to know to solve this problem?" "Let me think back to when we covered this information in class." "I'd better outline some ideas before I answer this one." "Am I moving fast enough to finish the test on time?"

| Timer ring | On-task | Off-task |
|---|---|---|
| 1. | _____ | _____ |
| 2. | _____ | _____ |
| 3. | _____ | _____ |
| 4. | _____ | _____ |
| 5. | _____ | _____ |
| 6. | _____ | _____ |
| 7. | _____ | _____ |
| 8. | _____ | _____ |
| 9. | _____ | _____ |
| 10. | _____ | _____ |

Pass out the self-monitoring sheet, and explain to your class that you want them to think about their thinking processes. They can begin by practicing on routine class assignments, rather than on an important test. Tell them:

> We do best in school when we are directly think-
> ing about our work and how to do it best. We don't
> do as well when we are thinking about how well

someone else is doing, or how well we might do,
or what we would rather be doing. Let's go over
some examples of what is "on-task" thinking, and
what is "off-task" thinking.

Read the examples on the self-monitoring sheet with the
class and discuss them. Question: Why is each instance an
example of "on-task" or "off-task" thinking? Review each
example. Be sure they understand that some thinking can
be *related* to the task (e.g., worrying about how well one is
doing) but not be "on-task." It can be directly helpful to
the successful completion of the task.

Give the students an assignment, and tell them, while
completing it, to listen for the timer to ring. Set the timer
for different intervals. When it rings, ask them to record
what they were thinking about when the timer rang and
evaluate whether it was "on-task" or "off-task". Revise
sheet to record their thoughts—share them with each
other in class discussion; decide whether on- or off-task.
Make sure that they know, at least at first, that the goal is
not to check "on-task" 10 times; rather, the goal is to
accurately evaluate their thinking. It is important for
students to believe the more accurately they monitor their
own thinking, the more they will be able to help themselves improve their test scores. Students' scores should
be kept confidential, but you may wish to compare these
test scores with what *you* think their level of off-task
thinking is.

If students appear to exhibit too much "off task"
thinking, they should consciously make themselves re-
turn to task, that is, use the type of "on-task" thinking
described in the self-monitoring sheet, above. Thoughts
like, "I can't do this," should be replaced with relevant,
positive, appropriate thoughts like, "What is the best way
to answer this question?" When students find themselves
concentrating on how low their test score may be, they

should begin to concentrate on whether they are using appropriate strategies for answering specific test items. If so, they should think positively about how they applied all the knowledge they had to get the best possible answer.

If students practice monitoring their thinking, they should begin to get better at keeping their thinking on task. One good way to do this would be to keep a chart which measures their percentage of on-task thinking over time. Students should learn to set goals for themselves and to feel personal satisfaction in making their thinking more efficient and goal oriented. The more students practice this type of self-monitoring, the more effective it will be. (See Lloyd & Landrum, 1990, for more details.)

*Relaxation.* If some students appear to have particular difficulty with physical tension in test-taking situations, relaxation strategies may be helpful in reducing this tension. For physical tension, a self-monitoring approach can also prove beneficial, using a similar self-monitoring sheet:

SELF-MONITORING SHEET
Relaxation

This sheet will help you monitor your level of tension or relaxation. Each time the timer rings, check whether you were "relaxed" or "tense." Here are some examples:

*Tense:* Grinding or clenching teeth. Tapping foot. Rapid paced, shallow breathing. Drumming fingers. Clenched hands. Tense muscles. Rapid heart beat. Tapping pencil. Sweaty hands. Fidgeting in seat. Picking at face or hair. Biting fingernails.

*Relaxed:* Relaxed but good posture. Relaxed muscle tone. Slow, deep breathing. Positive thoughts. Calm physical manner, with no 'nervous' behaviors, such as fidgeting, biting fingernails, or pencil tapping. Slow, relaxed heart beat.

| Timer ring | Relaxed | Tense |
|---|---|---|
| 1. | _____ | _____ |
| 2. | _____ | _____ |
| 3. | _____ | _____ |
| 4. | _____ | _____ |
| 5. | _____ | _____ |
| 6. | _____ | _____ |
| 7. | _____ | _____ |
| 8. | _____ | _____ |
| 9. | _____ | _____ |
| 10. | _____ | _____ |

This sheet can be used in the same way as the "on-task thinking" self monitoring sheet described. First, emphasize the necessity of answering honestly in order for it to help them do better in school. Then, have students practice filling it out, and compare their recordings with your observations. Have them chart their performance over time, and give them positive feedback for improvement. They should be made to understand that everyone gets tense at times, but that students who can observe tension in themselves and control it will have a better time in school.

Students who appear to be overly tense should practice doing the things listed under "relaxed" examples on the self-monitoring sheet. Anxious students can practice sitting still, taking a long, deep breath, keeping hands and feet free from unnecessary movement, and actively reducing muscle tension. Focusing thoughts on test-taking strategies, rather than anxieties (see above), can also help promote relaxation. (See Erwin & Dinwiddie, 1983, for relaxation exercises.)

It may also be helpful to practice breathing exercises with the class, so they may be more easily able to implement them when they find themselves becoming tense. Erwin and Dinwiddie, in their book *Test Without Trauma* (pp. 145-146), provide directions for a breathing exercise:

> ...Get into a very relaxed position...Now begin to pretend that your body is like a huge milk bottle. You are going to fill the bottom first. As you inhale slowly and deeply, allow your stomach to expand...Let your belly hang out and imagine that you are filling it with air. Then fill your chest, then your throat, and then your mouth. Keep inhaling. When you are as full of air as you think you can possibly be, hold it. Now, begin to exhale. Empty the bottom of the milk bottle first...empty your chest, your throat and your mouth until you have totally emptied your body of air. Now hold it...until you repeat the process.

Erwin and Dinwiddie recommend continuing the breathing exercise for five or ten minutes. When students undertake such an exercise, they should also try to clear their mind of anxious thoughts and simply concentrate on their breathing. They should learn to relax and breathe correctly when they begin to feel anxious while taking a test.

## IMPROVING MOTIVATION

When we think of motivation, we often think in terms of rewards. That is, the desirability of the reward is often associated with how hard we try. For instance, students who feel "rewarded" by high grades or teacher praise may be motivated to try hard on tests so they can receive these rewards. Such rewards are referred to as extrinsic motivation (Lepper & Hodell, 1989). On the other hand, some students may have little interest in high grades or teacher praise, or feel that they have little chance of scoring high enough to receive any acknowledgment.

Students such as these, low in feelings of "self-efficacy" (Schunk, 1989) may need additional incentives to work hard on tests.

## External Motivation

One way of improving motivation and effort is by directly rewarding improvement in test performance with privilege, tangible rewards, or even money (Lepper & Hodel, 1989; Taylor & White, 1983). If you use such externally provided incentives, however, be sure that such rewards do not violate standardized test administration procedures. It is also important to ensure that you are rewarding the student's effort, by comparing the student's current performance with previous performance(s), rather than by comparing students with each other. Finally, it is important to continue to express your own personal satisfaction for the increased effort. Encourage students to feel proud of themselves when they try hard.

## Internal Motivation

Students are likely to feel motivated when they feel that they are personally in control of those things they are expected to do. This is more likely to happen if you encourage the students to do things they can be in control of, rather than things they may not be able to directly control. For example, if a child is strongly encouraged to "be a great tennis player," he or she may become confused and frustrated because the child does not know what specific skills he or she needs to manage. However, if the child is encouraged to "always keep your eyes on the ball," such a direction specifies a behavior the child is potentially in control of, and encourages feelings of self-efficacy. Such encouragement may be more motivating for the child, who is able, with effort, to exhibit the desired behavior.

*Attribution.* Students with higher levels of motivation are those who attribute success or failure to their own success or failure in correctly applying their learned skills and strategies. They do not attribute success or failure to forces outside their control, like good or bad luck, or teacher bias. The more you can encourage attributions that suggest conrtol is vested in the student, the more likely your students will be to be motivated to achieve (Fulk, Mastropieri, & Scruggs, 1992; Schunk, 1989).

*Test-taking attributions.* When taking tests, exhortations to "score high," or "get the highest score in the class," may not lead to the expected results as your students may not feel in control of these things. Instead, when encouraged to concentrate, try hard, and execute specific strategies (such as checking work and saving hardest items until last), students are likely to feel in control of these behaviors, especially if they have practiced them. If students feel they are rewarded for executing specific skills to the best of their ability, they are more likely to work hard to achieve, than when unrealistic or poorly defined expectations are placed on them.

The best way to encourage your students' motivation is to be sure they are familiar with important test-taking skills, and both encourage and reward students for using these skills. Here are some examples of teacher comments that may be more positively related to student motivation:

Comments Which Encourage Appropriate Attributions

- "This is an essay test, so be sure to use the test-taking skills that you learned for taking an essay test."

- "Remember to answer every question, like we practiced."
- "If you relax, concentrate, and use on-task thinking, I'm sure you will get a score you can be proud of."

Here are some examples of encouraging inappropriate attributions:

Comments Which Encourage Inappropriate Attributions

- "Maybe you'll get lucky on the test today."
- "See if you can get the highest grade in the class on this test!"
- "Show us all what a great student you can be!"
- "This test is too easy for you!"
- "You should be getting straight A's in this class!"

Although such comments may be well-intentioned, they may not increase motivation or attitude because they concentrate on those things students may not feel in control of. Encouraging students to do things they feel that they can do is more likely to promote motivation.

By carefully evaluating your own comments to students, and encouraging them to use the skills and strategies they have learned, you can do much to improve your students' motivation.

## Summary

In this chapter, we have discussed academic preparation, physical preparation, attitude-improving, anxiety-reducing, and motivational strategies for improving test performance. These strategies were referred to as "general, all-purpose strategies," because they can be used in any testing situation. However, these strategies, to be truly effective, should be combined with strategies designed to be used with very specific test formats. These specific test-taking strategies are discussed in the chapters that follow.

# CHAPTER 4

# Taking Standardized Tests

Standardized tests have become a permanent feature of the educational enterprise. Unlike other types of tests, standardized tests serve to determine where a particular student stands with respect to a sample of students intended to represent students in general. Scores are recorded in terms of percentiles or grade equivalents — that is, what percent of students in the sample scored lower than the student in question, or what grade level of accomplishment does a given student's score represent.

Standardized tests are typically administered under highly controlled conditions so that students' scores can be fairly compared with students who took the test under those same conditions. Frequently, these conditions vary markedly from the situations students are accustomed to. The tasks themselves may be very different from classroom tasks familiar to students. Many students have little difficulty coping with these unusual conditions and novel tasks; however, there also exists a group of students who do have difficulty demonstrating their skills under these conditions. Such students can benefit greatly from training in test-taking skills.

In this chapter, we describe a variety of strategies which can be employed on standardized tests. We will first describe some overall strategies for standardized tests. Next, we will describe specific strategies for use on specific test formats, such as reading decoding, reading comprehension, math concepts, math computation, math problem solving, and content area subtests.

# GENERAL STRATEGIES FOR TAKING STANDARDIZED TESTS

The strategies described in this section can generally be applied across a variety of standardized tests, and include use of separate answer sheets, elimination strategies, guessing, and using time efficiently.

## Using Separate Answer Sheets

One of the most obvious characteristics of standardized tests is that students are asked to color in, with pencil, appropriate answer "bubbles," rather than provide written or oral answers to questions. In most cases, these answer bubbles are located on a separate sheet of paper, which can be easily scanned by computer, while the actual test booklet is not marked.

The overriding format of these tests is a stem and three or more options. The test-taker reads the stem, decides which of the options seems most likely to be correct, and colors in the answer bubble next to this option number or letter on the separate answer sheet.

Separate answer sheets are typically not provided to students in the primary grades as research has indicated that children in these grades lack necessary skills for using separate answer sheets. In our own research (Veit & Scruggs, 1986), we found that some older students, particularly those in special education programs, may also have difficulty with separate answer sheets. This difficulty may translate into lowered test scores, when correctly identified answer choices are colored in incompletely or in the wrong space even though the student may know the answer. Since few would argue that a student's ability to color in answer bubbles on a separate answer sheet should be a valid part of a reading or math test score, it seems appropriate to train students who may be lacking these skills.

## Strategies for using separate answer sheets.

*1. Placement of test booklet and answer sheet.* Some students experience difficulty maintaining their place on the test page or the answer sheet page. The consequence can be answers correctly marked on the wrong part of the answer sheet which will most likely be scored as incorrect answers.

**Tip: Have students fold test booklets and answer sheets so that only one page of each is showing—they will be less likely to lose their place.**

*2. Matching subtests and answer sheet.* We have frequently seen students correctly match numbers from the answer sheet and test booklet, but forget to check that the subtest in the test booklet matches the subtest on the answer sheet.

**Tip: Be sure your students' subtests in test booklets match those on the answer sheets.**

*3. Page turning.* If two pages get stuck together when turning, disastrous consequences can result.

**Tip: Teach your students to check the page number every time they turn the page.** This is especially true if students practice folding their test booklet, as recommended in #1 above. **When the booklet is folded, it must be turned over when the page is finished, and when the next page is finished, the page must be turned *and* the booklet turned over.** The practice of looking at one page at a time will not be helpful if careful page turning is not also practiced.

*4. Using both sides of the answer sheet.* This is true, of course, for answer sheets that are printed on both sides. Students may be tempted to stop working when they see the answer sheet filled.

**Tip: Show the students prior to the actual testing that the answer sheet has two sides, and they must go on to the second side when they finish the page.**

*5. Matching numbers carefully.* It is important that students always check that the test item number in the booklet matches the number they are marking in on the answer sheet. If the student inadvertently skips a test item, and does not skip the corresponding answer sheet item, all the following answers for that subtest will be marked in incorrectly. If the student discovers this mistake part way into the test, much valuable time will be lost tracking the original error.

We have also seen students start with the correct number, but then complete items *across* the answer sheet, when they should proceed *down* the answer sheet column.

**Tip: Practice helping the student carefully check each number before answering.**

*6. Marking the answer choice.* Answer choices must be marked completely so they can be accurately read by machine, and the marking must stay inside the answer space, to be recorded correctly. However, students must also work quickly to avoid wasting time marking the spaces. Some students believe none of the answer space can be allowed to show through, and spend too much time going over and over their marking.

Tip: Students should be taught that overly elaborate marking is unnecessary and takes time away from answering other questions.

7. *Checking answers.* Students should check not only the correctness of their answer choices, but also the correctness of their marking. If answer choices appear too light or stray far outside the line, these marks should be corrected.

*Practice.* You can provide practice for your students using simulated test booklets and answer sheets which are similar in appearance to the test they would be taking. Do not include any of the items that will appear on the test. So they can practice use of separate answer sheets only, indicate with an arrow the correct answer to each question on the students' test booklets, as in the example below:

1.  Which is the numeral for seven million, four hundred, three?

> a. 7,000,430
>
> b. 7,040,003
>
> c. 7,000,403 ←
>
> d. 7,004,003

Direct your students to mark the answer correctly on the separate answer sheet and give them instruction and practice in the strategies listed above. Many students should be able to substantially improve their performance after only a few practice sessions. Such activities, while probably not necessary for all students, can be of great help to some students and can help prevent major problems during actual testing situations.

If you yourself are administering the standardized test, you are probably allowed to actively encourage students to check their use of answer sheets, and monitor them to ensure they are on the correct subtest and correct item. Check the administration manual for specific information on how closely you can monitor students' use of answer sheets.

## Elimination Strategies

Elimination strategies on standardized multiple choice formats refer to strategies used when the exact answer is not known for certain. In such cases, if an answer is chosen at random, it stands as good a chance of being correct as any other answer option. That is, if there are four answer choices, it has a 25% chance of being correct (1/4). If there are three answer choices, the probability is 1/3, or 33%; for five answer choices, the probability is 1/5, or 20%.

However, it is often the case that the test-taker, although unsure of the exact answer, has *some* knowledge of the information being tested. Such partial information is used by good test takers, not necessarily to obtain a correct answer, but to eliminate less likely choices, decreasing purely random answering. Over a large number of items, when the answer is not definitely known, the good test taker stands to receive a higher score, overall, than the student who makes random choices. Test takers with partial knowledge deserve credit for this knowledge when it leads them to making a correct answer choice. On many standardized tests, two or three more questions answered correctly can make a substantial difference in the overall score.

Remember, multiple choice test questions do not require that students produce the correct knowledge — only that the student accurately identify an option as more likely correct than alternatives. There are two ways of doing this. One is to know with certainty that a specific option is the correct answer. The other is to know that all but one of the options is *not* likely the correct answer. Either type of knowledge is acceptable on multiple choice tests. We will be saying more about elimination strategies in the chapter on classroom tests.

## Guessing Strategies

Recently, we asked students why they chose their test answers (Scruggs, Bennion, & Lifson, 1985a, 1985b). We ordered these items in terms of their likelihood of being correct. The most likely reasons to be incorrect involved misreading the question or not following directions. For those most likely to be correct, students reported feeling certain that a specific option was correct ("I knew that was the answer"). In the middle range were a variety of specific strategies, some of which were format-specific and are described in the sections which follow. However, when students reported "guessing," or that a specific answer "sounded right," in that the answer seemed to strike a chord of familiarity, nearly 50% of the answers were correct. Although "sounded right" responses were more likely to be correct than "guessed," the actual differences are trivial.

This suggested that students often stand a very strong chance of answering correctly, even when they are not at all sure of the correct response. "Guessing" helps produce a correct answer. **Encourage students to guess whenever they feel unsure of an answer.** When time permits, they should read the stem and answer choices and think about the choices before answering. At worst they will answer a certain percentage correctly; at best, their "educated guesses" — that is, guessing in an area they have recently studied — will result in much higher scores than they may have imagined!

In some tests, there is a "penalty" for guessing. Typically, this means that incorrect choices are subtracted from correct choices in computing the score, while no credit is given for items left blank. When guessing is strongly penalized, it may be wise to avoid random guessing. However, even then, test-takers should try to make an educated choice. A "guess" with a good chance of being correct may be better than an item left blank. If you examine the scoring procedures and formats of tests with guessing penalties, you can help the student understand the extent to which guessing is penalized. But we recommend that "guessing" be generally encouraged.

## Using Time Wisely

In taking almost any test the *rate* at which test items should be answered is a critical consideration. Since most tests are timed, this usually involves dividing the number of test items by the amount of time allowed, and computing a rate at which the items should be answered. For example, if there are 60 items on the test, and one hour is allocated, test-takers should answer, on average, no less than one item per minute. Ideally, even more than one item per minute should be answered since one wants time left to check answers at the end. A test-taker should set a goal that after 15 minutes, 18 items should have been answered; after 30 minutes, 36 items; after 50 minutes, all items should have been answered, leaving ten minutes to check all previous work.

Such a computation assumes that all items are of equal difficulty. The student should first look over the entire test, and make a judgment regarding the relative difficulty of test items. If some items seem to need more time, students should adjust the rate they go through the items. In some cases, it may be helpful to answer such questions first, so that students can more carefully monitor their time throughout the test.

In some cases, there may be so many items that students must answer all items as rapidly as possible. Even in such cases, students should still try to leave time to skim through remaining items at the end of the test.

When time is very short, and there are many unanswered items, students should make a point to answer as many as possible, as fast as possible. If they don't answer, they will have no chance of earning points, but if they guess, at least some may be right. With some practice and encouragement, most students will find that improved time use will improve their test scores.

# STRATEGIES FOR TAKING SPECIFIC STANDARDIZED TESTS

When we trained students to become better test-takers, we found that the more closely our training resembled actual test formats, the more likely students were to profit from the training. We next discuss test-taking strategies specific to standardized achievement subtests in reading, math, and content areas.

Before we begin, you should know there are a great variety of test item formats on standardized achievement tests. There is also a great variety of difficulty levels since the tests span abilities from kindergarten to grade twelve. Although most standardized achievement tests contain reading comprehension subtests of the type represented here, the other subtests vary. Some tests use different formats for assessing reading decoding; others, particularly at the higher grade levels, do not assess decoding at all. Tests vary in whether they contain subtests on syllabication, science, social studies, referencing, or language expression.

Given this variability, it is not possible to provide examples for all the different formats which appear on current standardized achievement tests. Most standardized achievement tests, however, are more similar than they are different. Our overall recommendation: read carefully the sections which follow, examine the formats contained on the tests which your school administers at your students' grade level, and adapt our recommendations for those specific formats.

## Strategies for Reading Comprehension Tests

Most standardized achievement tests employ a similar format for assessing reading comprehension. This format typically consists of a short reading passage followed by several multiple choice questions concerning the passage. About three quarters of these questions require recall of information taken literally from the passage; about one quarter require an inference based upon information in the passage.

Several specific strategies can be helpful for students taking standardized reading comprehension tests which utilize this format. Some strategies we taught are listed below:

*1. Read as much of the passage as possible.* Train the student to read the passage through, regardless of whether they can read all the words!

Many students, particularly remedial or special education students, are used to reading under teacher supervision using controlled materials. They may not be well prepared for reading through passages which contain words they can not read, and receiving no teacher feedback or prompting. Other students read more independently, but still are likely to encounter passages beyond their reading level on achievement tests.

*STRATEGY:* Prior to the test, all students should practice reading passages at higher difficulty levels than they usually work with. They should be encouraged to continue to read past unfamiliar words to retain as much meaning as possible.

We found that, even with several difficult words omitted (and replaced with blank lines) from the passage, students were still able to derive meaning from the passage and answer many comprehension questions. We told the students the blank lines could stand for words they might not be able to read. We then showed them that passages could still be understandable, even if they could not read all the words.

The most important consideration with this strategy is that students do not give up reading the passage when they encounter difficult words. They should continue reading as many words as possible, and then see how many questions they can answercorrectly.

*2. Read each question and all answer choices.* Students have often been observed impulsively choosing an option which exhibits some superficial familiarity, without considering answer choices. Sometimes, they don't even read the question! Such an approach is only acceptable when there is little time left, and they are simply answering at random.

*3. Refer back to the passage to be sure your answer is correct.* In most cases, the answer to the test item is found directly in the reading passage. These items require direct *recall* of the specific information or the ability to recall where the information was mentioned. In a smaller number of cases, students are required to *infer* an answer from information given in the passage. Students should be provided with practice in determining whether items are likely to be recall or inferential items. In many cases, a recall item requires the identification of a specific detail ("Whom did Andrea call?"); while inferential items ask for an opinion, such as for authorship ("This paragraph was probably written by..."), or asks for a judgment about how a specific character felt about in the events in the passage ("How does the boy in the story feel?").

Checking the passage will also help confirm whether the answer is explicitly stated, or only alluded to. Students can be taught to find the relevant section of the passage, and make a judgment whether the answer is explicitly stated or not. If it is not stated, and the correct section of the passage is being examined, the reader is probably being required to make a judgment.

**Strategy:** Students should be shown how to gather evidence and choose among the response options. The response options themselves may help define what the student should look for.

Students who have received practice in approaching reading passages in this manner will more likely be able to cope with such formats in standardized achievement tests.

In some cases, a "passage" is not included at all, but instead a table, schedule, "note" or poem is substituted. This is done, presumably, to test the student's ability to "comprehend" different types of written material. Practice with such types of reading prior to the test is also likely to be helpful.

Schedules or tables which will require students to look up specific information demand focussed attention by the students.

**Strategy:** Students should be taught to briefly scan the information to determine what it is and how it is organized, and then to proceed directly to the questions.

What is important in such items is the student's ability to refer to the table to answer questions, rather than the student's immediate recall of a table or schedule which has just been read. For example, consider the following:

TEST EXAMPLE:

1991-1992 NORTHERN STATE UNIVERSITY
BASKETBALL SCHEDULE

*NOVEMBER*
Nov. 24    N.S.U. vs. **Western State**
           game time 7:00 pm
Nov. 26    **N.S.U.** vs. Eastern Indiana
           game time 7:30 pm

*DECEMBER*
Dec. 11    †N.S.U. vs. **South Bend State**
           game time 7:00 pm
Dec. 22    †N.S.U. vs. **Hammond University**
           game time 8:00 pm

*JANUARY*
Jan. 5     †**N.S.U.** vs. Elkhart State
           game time 8:00 pm (televised)
Jan. 12    †N.S.U. vs. **Fourier College**
           game time 7:30 pm
Jan. 28    **N.S.U.** vs. Great Lakes College
           game time 1:30 pm

†Northern Conference Games
**Home games in bold**

25. Which game is played in the afternoon?

      a. Hammond University

      b. Elkhart State

   * c. Great Lakes College

      d. Fourier College

26. Which game can you see on Dec. 22?

      a. Elkhart State

      b. Fourier College

   * c. Hammond University

      d. Eastern Indiana

27. What does the † stand for?

      a. home games

      b. away games

      c. games played in the afternoon

   * d. Northern Conference games.

28. Which game will be televised?

   * a. Elkhart State

      b. Eastern Indiana

      c. Fourier College

      d. Hammond University

Students should not waste unnecessary time trying to read and remember all the information in the table. Rather, they should skim the entire table to learn how to find information. When they feel certain they know how to *use* the table (rather than remember all the information on it), they should proceed to the questions and look up all the answers in the table.

## Strategies for Word Knowledge and Decoding Subtests

Decoding and word knowledge subtest formats are often different from the tasks students are familiar with and may be more likely to be misunderstood. The reason such formats appear unusual is that group-administered tests cannot ask students to read and decode specific words as an examiner can on individually administered reading tests. Group-administered tests may be answered in multiple choice format, or other formats in which students identify rather than produce the correct answer. This does not lend itself easily to tests of decoding or word-attack skills. In this section, we describe strategies you can teach your students for coping with vocabulary, syllabication, and decoding subtests.

*Vocabulary.* Vocabulary subtests vary in their formats, but one common format for group administered, standardized tests involves stating a vocabulary word, sometimes within a specific context, and providing answer choices, one of which is a close synonym for the vocabulary word. An example is given below:

14. A long **corridor**.

      (a) ruler

      (b) book

   * (c) hallway

      (d) river.

*The general strategy* most appropriate for this subtest is to read all answer choices carefully before choosing. In some cases, students may skip items such as this because they can not read one or more words in the stem or option. If the student can not read a word, or even guess at its pronunciation, students should make a "best guess" and move on. However, since most students can read at least some of the words in the item, they should be encouraged to study carefully the words they can read and try to identify the correct option. If they can not, they should be encouraged to use elimination strategies to improve the probability of answering correctly.

Another, less common type of vocabulary test item involves choosing a word that contains two different given meanings. For example:

22. *Green area around a house* and *36 inches*

        a. tree

        b. foot

   * c. yard

        d. bushes

This item calls for the student to choose the word that means both "green area around a house," and "36 inches." Students should read the stem, and then try each choice in both underlined sections to see if it makes sense. For example, in #22 above, students should ask themselves the following questions:

1.  Is a tree a green area around a house? Possibly, but is a tree 36 inches? No, so go to "b."

2.  Is a foot a green area around a house? No, so go to "c."

3.  Is a yard a green area around a house? Yes, but is a yard 36 inches? Yes, so "c" is *probably* the answer. Go to "d."

4.  Are bushes a green area around a house? Maybe, but are bushes 36 inches? No, so "c" is the answer.

A third type of vocabulary item requires students to read a short passage and identify the meaning of the under-lined word.

14.  The bell rang, and the students sat down. Ten minutes later, Judy came in, running. She was *tardy*.

  * a. late
     b. early
     c. tired
     d. happy

Students should read the passage and pick the answer choice that means the same as the word that is underlined in the passage.

**Tip: Students could be told to read each answer choice in place of the underlined word to see if it really is correct before choosing the answer.**

In many cases with such items, clues to the meaning are somewhere else in the passage. For example, if a student does not know what *tardy* means, the student should be encouraged to look over the known words, "the bell rang," "ten minutes later," and "running," and *infer* that tardy means late.

*Syllabication.* In syllabication subtests, students are asked to choose which of several options contains the correctly divided word. For example:

9.  Minimal:

      * (a) min-i-mal

        (b) mi-ni-mal

        (c) min-im-al

        (d) mi-nim-al

Teachers should, first, be certain that students who will be taking this type of subtest have had the opportunity for sufficient practice at syllabication. In this case, it is important to establish certainty that students have mastered specific rules for syllabication, and can apply them within this type of format. It is important to know, for example, that syllables are generally divided *between* two consonants, and *after* the consonant when syllable division occurs there. Students can also be given practice looking for smaller, semantically relevant words that are part of the larger word, as syllables are commonly divided there (e.g., fish-er-man; mail-box-es). Teaching these strategies is virtually the same as teaching the skill of syllabication. However, in this context, it makes little sense to test skills that have not been taught, and, as long as the practice examples are not the same as actual test items, such instruction is appropriate.

*Decoding.* Formats for decoding subtests on group-administered, standardized tests are typically very different from the decoding activities students receive in school. Usually, a stem is provided with an underlined sound. The test-taker is required to select the answer choice which has a sound most like the underlined sound in the stem, such as the following:

25. st<u>ay</u>

    (a) stand

    (b) tire

* (c) afraid

    (d) flag

Providing your students with some guided practice with this item type may be very helpful, as students probably have not approached decoding activities using such a format. If they have encountered this type of format, perhaps in a workbook activity, the similarity should be made clear.

Students should review and practice the pages in the workbook with these examples. It is also important to emphasize that it is the *underlined* sound of the word which must be matched. Our own research has shown that some students may be quick to jump at an answer choice which bears a superficial resemblance to the stem word (e.g., "stand" for "stay"), when the target *sounds* are not similar.

**Strategy: Students should sound out all the words carefully, paying attention to the highlighted *sound* in the stem.**

When they are not able to read all words, they should read the words they can read and identify the correct answer or use elimination strategies to deduce the correct answer, and so narrow the possibilities.

If they cannot read the target word or any of the answer options, they should, as with previously described subtests, make a "best guess" and continue through the test.

## Strategies for Math Computation Subtests

Formats used for math computation are usually relatively straightforward, but can vary. A commonly used format takes the following form:

22.  38          (a) 68
     +3          (b) 31
              *   (c) 41
                  (d) 51

For examples such as this, you should teach your students to use separate paper to compute the problem (unless expressly prohibited), and make sure their computed answer matches the answer choice exactly.

But remember, when students are using scratch paper, they must simultaneously manage scratch paper, test booklet, and answer sheet. Once students have computed the problem, they must identify the correct answer in the test booklet and then identify and mark the correct choice on the answer sheet.

Some students may have difficulty keeping their papers organized. They should practice these exercises in class prior to the test. It is very possible to correctly compute the solution to the problem, and then to incorrectly identify it in the test booklet, or color in the incorrect answer on the answer sheet.

In some cases, different formats are employed, for example:

6.   24 + 6 =
              (a) 84
              (b) 29
          *   (c) 30
              (d) 40

In such cases, it is common for a specific answer choice to match the answer that would be obtained if the problem were not done correctly. For example, if a student placed the six under the two of the 24, and computed the answer at 84, that answer might be represented in the answer choices.

Good teaching requires that students have been taught the key concepts associated with computation, and have practiced calculating the numbers in a variety of different formats. Many students who have learning problems, such as those in special education, are typically presented with a more restricted range of activities, to minimize confusion. Their standardized test score, however, will be compared with students who have practiced a variety of different formats. It is important, then, for all students to learn the range of problem formats if they are to be tested on standardized tests.

All students should be made aware that they should line up addition, subtraction, and multiplication problems vertically. If there are no decimal places, they should line numbers up to the right. If the numbers contain decimals, the decimal points should be lined up vertically.

Students should also be given sufficient exposure to the *vocabulary* of mathematics. Words such as sum, difference, product, and quotient should be clearly understood before taking a standardized math test. Consider the following example:

10. The product of 12 and 11 is closest to:

      (a) 100

   * (b) 120

      (c) 20

      (d) 1

Students who do not understand key vocabulary may have a difficult time with this item. Note that the stem calls for the nearest *estimate* of the answer, rather than the actual product of the two numbers.

*Strategy:* **1.) Students who have any difficulty with this kind of estimation should be encouraged to solve the problem first, then check which answer is closest. 2.) Students with a clear concept of "product" should easily be able to eliminate (c) and (d), and correctly guess between (a) and (b).** Such strategies are especially helpful when time is short.

*Another helpful strategy:* Determine what the *last* number in an answer might be. For example, consider the item:

12.  187 X 385 =
             a. 572
          * b. 71,995
             c. 69,385
             d. 94,460

If the test taker has determined that the last digit of the correct answer must be five, but is less certain of (or too short of time to compute) the other digits, elimination strategies can be used to narrow the choices down to numbers ending in 5, i.e., 'b' and 'c.' Even if more than one choice remains (and this is likely to be the case) this elimination strategy can increase the probability of correct answering.

## Strategies for Math Concepts Subtests

Number concepts subtests test knowledge of a variety of terms, vocabulary concepts, and specific skills, such as rounding. Again, effective teaching strategies, which employ a large vocabulary and a variety of formats when teaching mathematics, are the most helpful practices for this type of test. In addition, knowledge of key vocabulary, number value, and visual representation of fractions are very helpful. For example, consider the item:

1.  Which numeral has the highest value:
    a. seven
    * b. nine
    c. six
    d. three

This item really addresses the question, "Which is the biggest number: 7, 9, 6, or 3?" in a different way, and presumably tests whether students have mastered the concept underlying the question by asking it in a different way.

Again, teaching which incorporates vocabulary training and requires students to answer questions when presented in different contexts, is likely to be very helpful to students on tests such as this.

In addition, encourage students, when confronted with an item in an unfamiliar format or context, to ask themselves, "How else could you ask this question?" They can answer by replacing less commonly used vocabulary with more commonly used (by them) vocabulary, and rewriting problems in more familiar formats, such as in the restatement of the problem above. Stated in more familiar terms, they will be more likely to answer correctly. For another example, consider the following:

3.  Which set has both odd and even numbers?
    a. {9, 11, 15, 3, 5}
    b. {6, 10, 4, 2, 8}
    * c. {6, 10, 7, 1, 8}
    d. {23, 15, 3, 7}

This item could potentially confuse students who are aware of "odd" and "even" numbers, but are uncertain of the meaning of "set." If you teach students to actively reason through each item, and to temporarily set aside unfamiliar terms, they should be able to see that one of the four answer choices has both odd and even numbers, and that therefore "c" is the best choice.

Sometimes number concepts items may contain unfamiliar (or forgotten) symbols. In such cases, elimination strategies may be appropriate. Consider the following example:

19. To show that 196 is less than 210, we could write:

        a. 196 X 210

        b. 196 > 210

        c. 196 - 210

   * d. 196 < 210

If you have taught your students to be good test takers, they should not despair when confronted with even such an item, even though they are not familiar with "less than" and "greater than" symbols. By using the elimination strategy and knowledge of other symbols, they should be able to narrow down the possible choices to "b" and "d", therefore increasing the possibility of a correct guess from 25% to 50%. Furthermore, if they have been encouraged to actively reason through each problem, they may deduce that the "smaller" end of the symbol may represent the smaller value, and answer the question correctly.

Finally, students may be unfamiliar with the "box" symbol which seems to appear consistently on many achievement tests, in items such as the following:

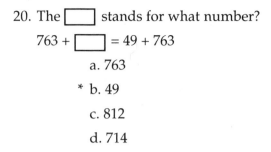

20. The ☐ stands for what number?

$$763 + \boxed{\phantom{xx}} = 49 + 763$$

       a. 763

    * b. 49

       c. 812

       d. 714

Students who have practiced with such boxes, and learned that the box stands for a number which is expected to be placed in the box, should not be confused with this item. Knowledge of the commutative property of addition (not necessarily by name) is seemingly required for answering this problem; however, students who are at least aware that neither adding nor subtracting 49 (choices "c" and "d") is appropriate will eliminate those choices. Some active reasoning should then put them in a position to answer correctly.

Many math concepts and problem solving subtests (or even math computation subtests) contain sentences which must be read by the test taker. Even though the reading level of these subtests may be lower than grade level, students with reading problems may find themselves at a great disadvantage. Check the administration manual of the test to determine whether you can help your students on the reading part of these items. If you are allowed to help with reading, pay close attention to students with reading problems during subtests which are not tests of reading skills, so that they do not lose valuable time waiting for reading assistance. **These students should be encouraged to ask for help promptly whenever they encounter an important word they can not read.**

## Strategies for Math Problem Solving Subtests

Many items in problem solving subtests are relatively straightforward word problems of the type encountered regularly in class. However, some of these problems require use of charts and graphs. It is important that students have practice and experience with these prior to taking a problem solving subtest.

Some problems may be complicated by, for example, items which ask test-takers to supply information which is not stated, but is nonetheless necessary to solve the problem. For example:

31. Fred is 63 inches tall. What else must you know to know how much he has grown in the past year?

    (a) How much he weighed a year ago

    (b) How tall he will be next year

    (c) How old he is this year

    * (d) How tall he was last year.

Students who have had practice with this type of problem are more likely to answer correctly than students who have not practiced this type of problem. In this particular item, a student could also use a "stem options" strategy to eliminate incorrect items. That is, since a measure of height is called for, measures of age or weight are not likely to be helpful information.

Students should also be taught to recognize when computation is required, and the necessary steps for computing an answer, as in the item:

8. Gerald paid $60.00 for a dozen baseballs. How much did he pay for each one?

      a. $10.00

      b. $5.00

      c. 12.50

      d. $6.00

Relevant strategies should parallel the strategies for computation subtests. All math strategies involve:

1. Reading the problem through and deciding on the correct operation(s);

2. Working out the problem on a separate sheet carefully, if necceary;

3. Writing the numbers carefully;

4. Checking your obtained answer against the choices;

5. Marking the correct answer choice; and

6. Answering correctly on the answer sheet (marking the correct space).

If the obtained answer does not match any answer option, and "none of the above" is not an option, students should check their calculations, and identify and correct their error.

## Science and Social Studies Subtests

Since the United States does not have a standard curriculum for science and social studies, test-makers are reluctant to ask specific recall questions concerning science or social studies content (e.g., "What was the Wilmot Proviso?", "What is an arthropod?"). Rather, standardized science and social studies tests often require students to extract meanings from scientific or social studies content provided in the test. These items often take the form of graphs, charts, maps, or reference materials. In addition, many items assess the student's ability to comprehend science or social studies content presented in anaccompanying reading passage. They are often similar to reading comprehension tests of science and social studies content.

Throughout the school year, students should be taught to extract meaning from a variety of graphic displays and tables in science and social studies content (such as relief maps, topographic maps, weather maps, maps of ocean currents, time lines of historical events, scientific tables and charts, population maps and charts), and answer questions based on these displays in a multiple choice format. Additionally, when they read passages describing science and social studies content, they should use the same strategies found in reading comprehension tests. Since the information contained in these passages is usually sufficient to answer questions, with sufficient practice and skill, they can be answered correctly. These are valuable exercises because students can come to understand that the strategies they used to answer some reading test formats can be used for readings whenever they occur on a test.

## SUMMARY

In this chapter, we discussed skills that can be used for taking standardized tests. These test-taking skills included general strategies, including use of separate answer sheets, elimination strategies, guessing strategies, time using strategies; and specific, format-driven strategies, including those useful for tests of reading comprehension, vocabulary, syllabication, decoding, math computation, math concepts, math problem solving, science and social studies. With careful attention to the general strategies given in Chapter 3 as well as the standardized test-taking strategies presented in this chapter, we feel certain that your students can receive their very best scores on these tests.

# CHAPTER 5

# Strategies for Classroom Tests

Classroom tests directly assess classroom learning. They are made by teachers, curriculum specialists or textbook publishers. While standardized tests provide important information on the grade-equivalent or percentile level of a student's academic functioning, compared with a national sample, classroom tests provide direct information on student mastery of classroom content. Acceptable performance on classroom tests is critical to school success, as up to 80% of a student's grade may be directly derived from classroom test scores. To demonstrate this knowledge, the student needs to understand the test-taking skills specific to these tests.

Classroom tests share many characteristics with standardized tests. Often, they are given with time limits using multiple choice or matching formats. Many of the strategies previously discussed apply to classroom tests. Classroom tests generally can be divided into objective tests and exams which require writing. Objective tests involve identifying the correct answer, and include such formats as multiple choice, matching, and true-false. Written exams require the student to produce the answers in essay, short answer or fill-in-the-blank formats. We discuss the test-taking strategies for these two types of classroom tests separately. A third type of classroom test, referred to as performance assessment, is gaining popularity in schools. This type of test, and the skills necessary to address it, is discussed at the end of this chapter. For additional information on strategies for classroom tests, especially for older high school and college students taking paper-and-pencil tests, we recommend the books written by Carman and Adams (1977) and Millman and Pauk (1969). Some of the material below is adapted from the latter book.

# OBJECTIVE TESTS

Objective classroom tests are more similar to standardized tests than exams which require writing. Several previously discussed test-taking strategies are highly appropriate. In addition to the general, all-purpose strategies such as academic preparation, physical preparation, attitude-improving, and anxiety-reducing strategies (discussed in Chapter 3), elimination strategies, guessing strategies, and time-using strategies (discussed in Chapter 4) are also very appropriate. In general, students should be taught to (a) use time efficiently, (b) read all directions and questions carefully, (c) attempt every question, and (d) actively think through each question. Materials and practice activities should be developed so that students can practice these strategies. For example, for effective time use, students should be able to examine a test with different sections and formats, and evaluate how much of the total test time should be spent on each section.

In addition to the above general strategies, strategies specific to answering objective types of test items should be taught, including the following:

## Strategies for Taking Objective Test Items

*1. Think of what the answer might be before reading the answer choices.* It may be helpful to have students think about the question for an instant before considering answer choices. If they do, they will be less likely to choose an attractive "decoy" answer. Although students may not think of exactly the answer provided, they can think of the domain of answers which the question calls for. For example, consider the question:

21. Radial symmetry refers to:

      a. Symmetrically placed bands of radioactivity in organisms.

      b. Physically similar leaf structure.

  * c. Similar body parts that extend out from the center of an organism.

      d. The characteristic of arthropods regarding specific stages of development.

If students think about the answer first, think actively of their knowledge of radial symmetry, and the context(s) in which they studied it, they are less likely to be misled by an answer choice such as 'a', which bears some superficial resemblance to stem vocabulary.

**2. Carefully consider all answer choices.** As the next step, they should carefully proceed through all answer options. Because many students, and particularly special education students, frequently jump at the first plausible option, test makers may place an attractive decoy prior to the correct answer. This will not prove to be a problem if the students examine all items individually. Teach students that even if they have identified a plausible answer choice, a *more* plausible choice may remain among items they neglected to read.

**3. Use elimination strategies.** Students should use logical reasoning to eliminate unlikely alternatives when the exact answer is not known for certain (see also Chapter 4). Use of partial knowledge and elimination strategies can increase the probability of a correct response. For example, consider the question:

16. The "Whisky Rebellion" occurred as a result of:

    (a) Objection to Jefferson's embargo

    (b) British occupation of distilleries

\*  (c) Washington's taxation policies

    (d) Westward expansion into Indian Territory.

If the student knows, for example, that the Whisky Rebellion took place during Washington's administration, he or she could choose between (c) and (d), improving the probability of a correct response from 25% to 50%.

*Practice.* You can practice elimination strategies by providing your students with practice tests. Initially, you may wish to begin with items from the "test-taking skills test" in the Appendix (particularly, with the "Absurd Options" items. This will help them with the general procedures for eliminating known incorrect answers. Later, when students have become familiar with elimination strategies, you can practice with "real" test items, in which elimination strategies are used when students do not know the correct answer, but nonetheless know that one or more options are likely to be incorrect.

Students can be questioned during activities in multiple choice format. When students do not know a correct answer, they should be asked to indicate the choices they know are incorrect and eliminate them. They then know to choose the correct answer from those that remain. Students should be rewarded for making a correct choice. Next we present some examples, one taken from one of the "Absurd Options" items in the Appendix, and one "real" item, for which students may have different levels of knowledge:

Teacher: "Class, I want you to look at this test item [shows item on overhead projector]:

3.  The Civil War hero, Lester McKellips:

> a. shot down many enemy planes
>
> b. led a successful charge against Confederate forces
>
> c. captured many German soldiers
>
> d. repelled a major tank offensive.

"Before you say anything, let me ask this question: Does anyone know who Lester McKellips is? [student responds, "The item says he was a Civil War hero."] Right, the item says that, but we don't know anything else about the person, do we? But, we do know something about the Civil War, and we can use this information to improve our score on the test.

"So, answer these questions: Were there airplanes in the Civil War? [Class responds]. Were there Germans? [Class responds]. Were there tanks? [Class responds]. Were there Confederate forces? [Class responds]. Yes, there were. So, we know the correct answer is probably 'b', because we can eliminate the others as not from the Civil War. We don't *know* the answer is correct, because we don't know who Lester McKellips is, but 'b' seems like the most likely choice.

"So you can look at choices that might *not be* correct, the same as you can look at choices that might *be* correct. In that case, it was just practice, as there really wasn't any Lester McKellips. Let's try it on a real item. Don't answer if you know the correct answer, but if you don't, let's see how close you can get [shows item on overhead projector]:

6.  The Confederate Officer "Jeb" Stuart:

> a. was criticized for his performance at Gettysburg.
>
> b. had been a decorated soldier in the American Revolution.
>
> c. played a major role in the Siege of Vicksburg.
>
> d. surrendered with Jefferson Davis at Appomatox Court House.

"Now, if you don't know the answer for sure, let's see if there are any we can eliminate. How about 'a'? [No response]. No, I don't think we can eliminate that one just yet. What about 'b'? [Student responds]. That's right, it can't be 'b' because a decorated soldier from the Revolution would be too old to be an officer in the Civil War. How about 'c', can we eliminate that? [Students respond]. No, that answer might be possible. Can we eliminate 'd'? [Student responds]. That's right, Jefferson Davis didn't surrender at Appomatox Court House, it was Lee. So we can eliminate 'd.' That leaves us with 'a' and 'c'. Now, does anyone know which Confederate army Stuart was with? [Student responds]. That's right, Lee's army, in the East. So if you know that, you know he couldn't have been at Vicksburg, which is in the West on the Mississippi River, since the Battle of Gettysburg happened at about the same time. So, the answer must be 'a', even though we don't know he was criticized for his actions at Gettysburg.

"Now, even if we didn't know Stuart fought in Lee's army, we could still eliminate two choices. So that would give us a 50% chance of answering correctly, rather than a 25% chance if we had just guessed. So you see how you might know more than you think you do."

5. *Consider "specific determiners".* Statements which contain the words "always" and "never" (rather than, for example, "usually" or "rarely") should be taken literally. Most of the time, items like this are false, since there are few statements that allow for no exceptions. However, they are not *always* false. Students should consider carefully the intention of the test as well as the content being tested (see also Chapter 4).

6. *Consider "stem options" and compare answers with each other.* Question stems which bear a strong logical relation to a specific answer choice, based on partial knowledge of the test taker, may be the most likely correct answer. For example, consider the item:

11. An important use of pyrite is:

      * a. the manufacture of acid;

        b. fooling mining investors;

        c. decoration and display;

        d. development of alloys.

The answer to this question should be limited to uses of pyrite considered (at least by the test author) to be important. On this basis, a minimal amount of prior knowledge could help the test-taker eliminate "b" and "c" as not particularly important, given that there is sufficient information to believe "a" or "d" may be correct.

Likewise, students should consider how answer choices compare with each other. Choices which seem absurd, given partial content knowledge, or two choices which seem to be stating the same information in different ways, can be eliminated, if other choices seem more likely.

Teach students to use these strategies to generally "reason through" difficult or less familiar information, and choose the option that overall seems to make the most sense.

## Strategies Which Should Not Be Taught

There are a number of test-taking strategies for objective classroom tests, occasionally successfully used by students, which you should *not* teach. These strategies, first identified by Jason Millman and Walter Pauk (1969), rely entirely upon flaws in test construction (Metfessal & Sax, 1968), and can be found in teacher-made tests, when the teacher has had little formal training in writing tests. Appropriate multiple choice distractors (that is, the two to four items which are not correct, but which should not be easily identified as incorrect) can be difficult to construct, and often contain flaws. Poorly constructed tests often contain cues in test items which students can use to their advantage. For example, on poorly constructed tests, items with the following characteristics provide cues to the correct answer:

Cues from Flawed Item Construction

Answers likely to be correct:

1. The *longest* answer,

2. The most *carefully qualified* answer,

3. An answer which contains familiar, appropriate vocabulary.

Answers likely to be incorrect:

1. The *first* or *last* answer choice,

2. Answers which contain extreme words, such as "stupid,"

3. Answers which appear flippant or absurd.

Here is an example of such a flawed item:

19. James Strang was:

> a. a Mennonite
>
> b. a Jew
>
> \* c. a Mormon dissident who founded the Strangite sect and started a settlement in an island in Lake Michigan;
>
> d. a Quaker.

You can see in item 19 above that option "c" is much longer and more carefully written than the other options. Although this is an exaggerated instance, teachers who are unskilled in writing multiple-choice test items may be prone to make this type of error.

Three arguments can be used against teaching such cues (see also Millman & Pauk, 1969). First, students can almost always use their time better by carefully examining the content of the test items. Second, students should be aware that "guessing" on the basis of *any* partial knowledge is generally better than presuming there is a flaw in the test item. Finally, developing reliance upon such strategies could prove detrimental when taking standardized objective tests, which contain few, if any, of such flaws. Remember, the purpose of training in test-taking skills is to help the student demonstrate his or her knowledge more effectively by understanding and applying strategies that enable effective test-taking. Teaching students to use "tricks" for correctly guessing the answers is not an appropriate purpose of test-taking skills training. In fact, if you find that some teachers produce consistent flaws in the tests they construct, you should alert those teachers so they can correct them. If you are teaching students to more effectively take *your* tests, it makes little sense to teach them how to cope with flaws or idiosyncracies in your own test construction (e.g., you rarely if ever make "none of the above" a correct answer choice). The best overall strategy is to eliminate the flaws in your own and other teachers' tests, and ensure that students are able to take well-constructed tests as efficiently as possible.

# WRITTEN TESTS

Written tests are the most difficult tests for students who have little knowledge of the content. In fact, these students should not expect to do well on tests, regardless of their knowledge of test-taking skills! However, our assumption in this book is that all students have studied, have some content knowledge, and can be trained to apply this knowledge more effectively on tests. Strategies appropriate for taking sentence completion, short answer and essay questions, are described separately below:

## Sentence Completion Items

Sentence completion items typically consist of the subject and verb of a content-relevant sentence, with predicate information left blank. Test-takers are required to fill in the blank space, thus completing the sentence. Strategies appropriate for sentence completion items include:

*1. Guess if unsure.* Sentence completion items rarely involve a penalty for incorrect answers, and students may be closer to the correct answer than they think.

*2. Use partial knowledge.* Students should respond to a sentence completion item with information they do have. For example, consider the item:

11. Near the end of the 17th century, Huguenots had their freedoms revoked by _____ (answer: Louis the XIV).

An answer which reflects some knowledge, as "the French King," even if not technically correct, may nonetheless earn partial credit. Another example:

6.   *Fathers and Sons* was written by _____ (Answer: Turgenev).

If the student did not know the name of the author, but could answer "a Russian novelist," such an answer may earn partial credit, and is better than no answer at all. The answer given, of course, must reflect *some* specific knowledge of the question. An answer such as "a writer" will not only earn no credit, it will convey to the teacher that the test is not being taken seriously. Another example:

21. Constantinople fell to the Turks in _____ (answer: 1453).

If the exact answer is not known, an answer such as "the 15th century" may earn partial credit. On the other hand, if the student knows the teacher requires precise dates, he or she should attempt a "best guess" answer.

*3. Make the sentence sound logical and consistent.* This consideration is similar to the "stem options" strategy for multiple choice tests. In sentence completion items, the part of the sentence that is presented may contain cues which restrict answer options. For example, in the following item:

8.   The overriding cause of the Civil War was

_____.

Students should limit possible answers to one considered (by the test maker) to be in some way "overriding." This cue should help eliminate possible alternative answers.

Other possible cues useful for such items include use of grammatical cues and consideration of the length of the answer blank, when appropriate. These cues, however, would only be taught as they interact with any partial knowledge of the content of the test item. For example:

3.   A frog is an example of an _____.

Students who are aware that a frog is not an arthropod, but are debating between reptile and amphibian may choose the latter, because of the anticipated initial vowel sound in the answer (<u>an</u> vs. <u>a</u>).

# ESSAY TESTS

In general, essay questions are the most difficult to answer, and there is, as with any other type of test, no substitute for knowledge of the content. However, it is rare that students are presented with a test question for which they have absolutely *no* information. The four parts of a general strategy for answering an essay question can be combined into the acronym **SNOW**, to help your students remember the four steps they should undertake in answering all essay test questions:

(1) <u>S</u>tudy the question,

(2) <u>N</u>ote important points,

(3) <u>O</u>rganize the information, and

(4) <u>W</u>rite directly to the point of the question.

If students wish to SNOW (i.e., impress) their teachers on their essay tests, then, they should do the following:

*1. Study the question.* Make sure your students realize that the best-written answer to a test question is useless if it does not directly address the question. If there are different parts or subquestions in a question, those must be addressed directly, so students should carefully note when multiple sections are called for in an answer. For example, in the question:

4.  What was President Jackson's policy toward the Cherokee Indians of the Southeastern United States? How did he defend that policy?

the student is expected not only to describe a particular policy, but also to describe how it was justified. Any answer which does not address both parts of the question would not receive full credit. By underlining or highlighting, students can remind themselves to attend to both parts of the question.

Teach students to underline or circle **command** words in the question to help direct the answer. As shown below, different command words convey very different meaning regarding how questions are to be answered. Students must also determine exactly how the teacher means these words to be interpreted. Teach your students to be aware of the question, but also how the question is to be answered.

## Command Words on Test Items and Their Implications

| *Word* | *Possible Implications* |
| --- | --- |
| Discuss | Provide reasoning behind, give different points of view. |
| Describe | Give an overall impression; give examples. |
| Compare | Show how two or more things are similar; provide examples of common characteristics. |
| Contrast | Show how two or more things are different; provide examples of differing characteristics. |
| Explain | Clarify or simplify; describe the rationale behind. |
| Justify | Argue in favor of; defend. |
| Critique | Argue in opposition of; find fault with. |
| List | Give a simple list of elements. |
| Outline | Give a list of elements organized into a system. |

Also, the question often provides cues on the expected length of the answer. For example, consider the item:

7.  In the space below, briefly list the findings of the Lewis and Clark expedition.

This item apparently requires only a short, and perhaps a not necessarily detailed, list. The expected length of the list may be further cued by the size of the "space below." Students who happen to know quite a bit more about the Lewis and Clark expedition may be tempted to write this information. However, a longer-than-expected answer is not only unnecessary, it can take time away from answering other questions. In most cases, when teachers want students to provide detailed or lengthy answers, they ask for detailed or lengthy answers.

*2. Note important points.* As students read the essay question, they should quickly jot down the first points that occur to them. They should note any point of merit that occurs to them; the order or relative importance of the point is not a major concern here. Often the first few minutes spent thinking about the test questions provide the best opportunities for recall of factual information. As students begin to tire later in the test period, time is better spent organizing or elaborating the answers than attempting to retrieve additional factual information.

*3. Organize information before writing.* Once facts about each question have been noted, students should organize these facts prior to writing. First, students should look through the list of points and identify those of major importance. Secondary points should be included under appropriate major points. They should then decide the order in which these points should be best presented.

*4. Write directly to the point of the question.* After organizing information, students should directly answer the major stated purpose of the question in the first sentence. The remainder of the answer should be devoted to providing directly supporting evidence to the answer, and should be written in a clear, concise, and well-organized form.

A sample lesson for teaching the "SNOW" strategy is given in the last chapter of this book.

**USE OF GENERAL STRATEGIES.** In addition to the "SNOW" strategy for answering essay test questions, students should keep in mind more general test-taking strategies which can also be applied to essay questions. These include the following:

*1. Answer every question.* Often, the test-taker has only partial knowledge of the questions. Since examiners nearly always give partial credit for partial information, your students should provide what relevant information they do know, and move on to the next question. However, they should avoid the temptation to provide information that they do know if it is not directly relevant to the particular question. Long-winded answers which provide factual information not being asked for are not usually helpful. Furthermore, writing off the point can take time away from directly answering other questions.

*2. Use time wisely.* Students should schedule enough time to answer each question. This can be helped by using the first two parts of the SNOW strategy, read questions carefully and note major points, for all questions before outlining and writing the answers to any of them. Once all items have been read and major points noted, students should divide their time more or less equally (depending on the expected length of the answers) among the questions. If time begins to run out, however, students should answer remaining essay questions using outline form and the points already noted. Since most teachers evaluate number of important points covered, such answers may still earn credit.

*3. Write or print neatly.* Such considerations as neatness and legibility of handwriting can be of critical importance in maximizing a test score. Your students should not spend so much time with neatness that time is lost for answering questions; however, since teachers can not grade answers they can not read, a minimal standard of legibility is of critical importance. Students with illegible cursive writing can consider printing answers. Such practice is commonly allowed in testing situations, and the teacher is likely to be thankful not to have to waste time deciphering illegible handwriting.

# PERFORMANCE ASSESSMENTS

Partly out of concern that traditional "paper and pencil" tests were not providing complete information on student knowledge, skills, and abilities, performance assessments have begun to gain in popularity.

## Characteristics and Implications for Teaching

Performance assessments can be conducted in all academic areas, and can involve a wide variety of tasks. Basically, the principle behind performance tests is that they test what the student can actually *do* (or "perform"), in contrast to displaying the shallower verbal knowledge commonly found on traditional tests. A performance assessment of writing, for example, would require that a student write something of relevance. A performance test in mathematics may involve "real world" problem solving activities involving numbers. Baron (1990) listed several advantages of performance assessment, including (a) improvement of instruction, (b) more valid information on skills and abilities society values, (c) integration with curriculum, (d) development of performance standards, and (e) informing policy decisions. Although infrequently used in schools today, the use of performance assessment is growing.

Performance tests can be implemented in varying degrees, from an individual student making measurements from a thermometer and a scale, to a group of chemistry students planning and executing a chemistry experiment, over a period of several days (Baron, 1990). It is part of our general principle that teachers should carefully consider the type of tests students will be taking when planning their instructional materials and instructional strategies. In the present case, it makes little sense to have students read in textbooks and complete worksheet activities if they are going to be assessed on their ability to manipulate and solve problems with real world materials.

Since these tests are typically meant to inform instructional practice, it seems clear that, if performance assessments are being used, the best strategies to use as a teacher to enhance student performance are to (a) teach to broad, general principles and conceptual understanding rather than emphasizing individual facts, (b) provide as many direct, concrete experiences with the phenomena being studied as possible, and (c) continuously monitor and prompt for understanding and the ability of students to apply principles generally, in many alternative instances. Far from being "test taking skills," these strategies simply constitute elements of effective teaching, and prompting teachers to use these strategies is part of the point of performance assessment.

## Test-Taking Skills for Performance Assessments

Since performance assessments are typically intended to be smaller pieces of the actual curriculum, applied in realistic situations, fewer test-taking skills may be necessary. In fact, many of the test-taking skills described in this book represent an attempt to help learners cope with confusing test formats that do *not* represent the medium or activities of instruction. Nevertheless, some of the overall principles of test-taking skills can be applied on these tests (physical and mental preparation, anxiety reduction, using time wisely), as well as some new skills for dealing with some of the unique properties of performance assessments. These strategies include:

*1. Read or listen to the directions carefully.* Since familiar, manipulative materials are often used in performance assessments, students may get the mistaken impression they know what is required of them, based on how they have interacted with these materials in the past. It is critical that students read or listen carefully to the directions, and question the teacher or examiner if there is any doubt whatsoever about what is to be done. For example, in a science performance assessment, a student may be presented with a variety of minerals, and be asked to perform specific tests (e.g., does a fingernail scratch it, does it "fizz" in vinegar, does it float?) to identify the minerals. Although some allowance may be made for "creativity," students who have a clear understanding of the anticipated outcome (identify the minerals), and the expected means to achieve the outcome (perform these tests) will be more likely to receive full credit.

*2. Talk through activities, if allowed.* The purpose of many performance assessments is to obtain a stronger measure of whether students have acquired relevant concepts, not simply that they have performed specific tasks. If a student understands the principles (electrical circuits), but has difficulty performing the required manipulation (e.g., use of wire strippers), talking through the task may indicate to the examiner that the important principles have been learned (e.g., "If I could ever get the insulation stripped off the ends of this wire, I would insert it in that clip to complete the circuit"). One present advantage of performance assessments is that they are flexible and responsive to the needs of the individual student.

This flexibility can be used effectively to understand what the student knows and so maximize the student's score.

*3. Use group interaction skills when needed.* Many of the performance assessments being discussed currently employ group performance or problem solving as one segment of the assessment. If this is the case, students should have received practice and instruction in group interaction of the type required on the assessment. Students should be very certain of what the group goals are, the roles of all group participants should be clarified, and criteria for meeting the goals should be identified. When individual group members go off-task, or conversely, take on too much responsibility, students should be able to use socially acceptable means of encouraging individual members to assume their appropriate role. Such strategies ideally would have been determined and applied in classroom activities involving group processes.

## SUMMARY

In this chapter, we have discussed a number of strategies that you can teach to students to help them increase their scores on teacher-made tests. We described specific strategies for objective, multiple-choice tests, as well as strategies for taking sentence completion, short answer, and essay tests. Overall, we tried to emphasize that students should be taught to consider all the general test-taking skills, as well as strategies specific to individual test formats. Although there is no substitute for comprehensive knowledge of the content being tested, we nonetheless maintain that training in test-taking skills is very important in helping students maximize their performance.

But how should such training be undertaken? Now that we have thoroughly covered test-taking skills relevant to a variety of testing situations, we will provide a description of how we think these skills should be taught. We address this issue in the next chapter.

# CHAPTER 6

# The Test-Taking Skills Curriculum

In the preceding chapters, we have presented the types of strategies that will help facilitate performance on tests, or "help students show what they know!" This chapter is intended to provide a model for teaching these strategies using the effective instruction model. First, the factors that teachers can use while teaching students are presented as part of this model. The second section indicates how the model can be applied to teaching test taking skills. The last section provides examples of lessons using some test-taking strategies discussed in earlier chapters.

## THE EFFECTIVE INSTRUCTION MODEL

Over the past decade teaching behaviors have been identified that increase the amount of information students learn. All of these behaviors are directly related to specific factors that teachers can manage. Each of these is described separately below.

### Time on Task

**The more time spent directly engaged in learning about or practicing the particular test-taking strategy, the better students will learn and perform that strategy.** Researchers have noted that teachers typically allocate more time for tasks than is actually used working on those tasks. It is important to increase the amount of actual engaged time on task for students. Time on task is the amount of allocated time versus engaged time on task during instruction. Teachers can tape record their instructional lessons, recording the amount of time students spent working on the assigned objective(s) for that lesson. It should be fairly easy to determine how the allocated time for the lesson compares with the engaged time.

It is useful to analyze what types of activities occurred that were considered "off task", or not related to student achievement of the instructional objectives. The following are examples of "off task" behavior:

(a) worksheets or other practice activities that are not directly relevant to lesson objectives;

(b) classroom management, such as disciplining students, awarding points or tokens, or taking attendance;

(c) transitional activities, such as passing out paper, pencil sharpening, and general classroom announcements; and

(d) student or teacher digressions or other verbalizations that are not directly relevant to the instructional objective.

In the case of test-taking skills training, engaged time on task would include time directly spent on teacher explanations, class discussions, and completion of guided and independent practice activities directly relevant to the acquisition of test-taking skills.

We have listed a variety of ways that teachers can increase the amount of engaged time on task in our book *Effective Instruction for Special Education* (1987). Some of those suggestions include careful planning of activities that can be commonly called "transitional time activities". With prior planning, teachers can require that students take care of tasks such as pencil sharpening and rest room breaks at designated times rather than in the middle of instructional lessons. Teachers can also be more prepared with classroom materials that need to be distributed to students throughout the class period.

## Content Covered

Another critical variable is the amount of content covered. If content is not covered, students will not have had the opportunity to learn the information. If content is covered too rapidly, students may not have the opportunity to master the information sufficiently. The length of the school year, school day, and academic period influence how instructional time is allocated to content objectives in a school year.

Teachers need to develop a clear scope and sequence for proposed content, and then identify which objectives in that scope and sequence need to be mastered. Time to teach test-taking skills should be included early in the school year since students are required to take tests throughout the academic year. Including test-taking strategies instruction on teacher-made tests at that time enables students to practice and apply them throughout the year. Since standardized tests are typically administered in the spring, training for taking these tests should take place several weeks prior to the administration of those tests.

Teachers should estimate the pace at which they need to move through the content on weekly, monthly, and marking term periods. The pace refers to the rate at which instruction occurs in the classroom, whether daily or in weeks. Pace, therefore, is directly related to the amount of content covered, whether in class or homework. At a minimum, teachers should monitor their progress or pace on a monthly basis. Periodic reviews of previously learned information should be incorporated to help students maintain their previously acquired skills and knowledge.

## Delivery of Instruction

The effective delivery of instruction refers to the activities teachers use to present information to students. These, in turn, have been shown to influence the amount of information students learn and retain. A common recommendation is that teachers teach to one objective at a time and provide many instances of the information which support what is being taught, and instances that do not. Negative mistakes help students define more clearly what is and is not relevant. Questioning techniques that involve many students provide them with multiple opportunities to practice learning the new information. We have suggested specific procedures for teachers to use in providing feedback to students when they have learned the material correctly, partially, or do not show understanding. Guided practice activities should be incorporated with lessons to provide students with opportunities to practice the newly acquired skills under careful guidance initially, and then with more independence. Finally, teachers should use formative evaluation procedures to collect information regularly on students' performance and progress on the instructional objective(s). This information can be used to monitor and adjust instruction based upon student progress. These factors are important and are now discussed in more detail.

*Teacher presentation.* Lessons typically begin with teacher presentation of the relevant information. This presentation should be clear, direct, and provide information that is directly relevant toward the lesson's instructional objective. Lessons should be structured to obtain and maintain student attention and motivation while simultaneously covering important information. An enthusiastic teacher presentation can kindle and maintain student interest and involvement. Teachers should provide activities for active participation on the part of all students.

These activities can include opportunities for choral responding, written responding, or combinations of those types of activities.

*Questioning and feedback.* Teachers should provide many questions for students to respond to, whether they are specific to restating rules or require higher level answers. For example, in learning the procedures for marking answers on separate answer sheets, it may be helpful to simply ask students "What is the best way to fill in the circles on answer sheets?", and to expect the rule response of: "quick, dark and inside the lines." Other times it may be more appropriate to ask higher level questions. For example, teachers might ask: How is studying for your social studies test different from studying for your science test? In this type of question, students would be expected to compare and contrast the two types of studying procedures and explain the rationale for each.

The type of feedback that teachers can provide students can vary depending upon the type of response given by students. Teachers should be overt in their feedback to students, so that students will know when a correct response has been given. Overt feedback may consist of repeating the correct response, praising the students with statements such as: "that's good, you seem to understand this test-taking strategy well," or simply smiling or nodding in affirmation. Feedback to partially correct responses should acknowledge the correct component of the response and provide prompts to the remaining unanswered component(s). If that fails, teachers may want to restate the question, as it may have been ambiguous, or they may want to allow another student an opportunity at responding. Feedback to incorrect responses can consist of statements referring to the fact that the answer was incorrect. Rewording the question may be beneficial, as the student may have misinterpreted the question. Feedback is a very important component of the delivery of instruction, as it is the opportunity for teachers to see what students really have learned from the lesson and more importantly, it allows students to know how they are doing.

*Guided practice.* Guided practice activities are opportunities for students to receive immediate corrective feedback about their performance during the lesson. During guided practice activities, the work is directly relevant to the instructional objective. Teachers can actively involve all of the students or most of the students all of the time. This is the ideal time for teachers to monitor and to verify whether or not students have caught on to the objective of the lesson. Teachers should provide guided practice prior to independent practice, as students should not be allowed to practice information independently if they do not know how to proceed. An example of guided practice on a test-taking skills lesson would be sample test items relevant to the test-taking strategy being taught, which the teacher and students work to answer together.

*Independent practice.* Independent practice follows the guided practice activity. Again the activity should be relevant to the instructional objective. This time students are provided with the opportunity to firm up their knowledge on the content covered during that lesson by applying it without teacher support — only feedback from the teacher or their classmates or both. Independent practice assists in building accurate and more rapid responding, and even "automatic" responding. Such activities can include paper-pencil tasks, practice on the computer, or opportunities to work cooperatively with peers either collaboratively or in a peer tutoring configuration where each partner takes a turn as student, then teacher. In a test-taking skills lesson, independent practice could require responding to specific test items testing the students' ability to answer using the test-taking strategies recently taught, which students answer independently.

*Formative evaluation.* Formative evaluation procedures gather information in an ongoing fashion throughout the school year. Instead of waiting until the end of the unit, chapter or term to give a test, teachers collect continuous measurements on students' work in order to monitor progress. Short quizzes help the teacher assess which students are mastering the skills or content, and which students are not. Teachers can then make effective instructional decisions by:

(a) maintaining instruction as is;

(b) providing more review;

(c) altering one or more instructional factors (e.g., increasing engaged time-on-task);

(d) increasing or decreasing the pace of instruction.

When training test-taking skills, teachers should collect information, not necessarily on items answered correctly on practice test items, but rather on the proportion of times the test-taking strategy was correctly executed.

## The Model for Daily Lessons

All of the variables listed above can be successfully incorporated into a teacher effectiveness model in the following way:

(a) Teachers should begin each lesson with a daily review of what types of content they have previously covered relevant to the objective(s).

(b) During this review teachers can help students activate their prior knowledge concerning the objective for the present lesson.

(c) Following the review, teachers should present the new objective for the present lesson.

(d) During this time the teacher presentation variables discussed above can be incorporated within the presentation. This is the time when all information presented should be directly relevant to the instructional objective.

(e) Following the teacher presentation are the guided practice activities. This is the time for teachers to guide and to monitor students' responses closely and provide corrective feedback and praise.

When students have demonstrated a sufficiently high level of correct responding and understanding, they are provided with the independent practice activities where they can firm up their understanding of the content presented in the lesson. Finally, the teacher can collect a short measure of the students' performance by administering the formative evaluation measure, e.g., an exercise embodying the test-taking skill. The results can be used to make effective instructional decisions regarding the instruction for future lessons.

The following format below can be used as a general guideline in designing lessons.

### Daily Lesson Components

1.  Daily Review
2.  Teacher Presentation (including statement of objective)
3.  Guided Practice
4.  Independent Practice
5.  Formative Evaluation

Unless there is an explicit reason otherwise, all lessons should follow generally this format.

# EFFECTIVE INSTRUCTION OF TEST-TAKING SKILLS

## The Curriculum

The entire model just described can be used to instruct students in test-taking skills. The following provides an example of a possible test-taking skills curriculum, as outlined in previous chapters in this book.

I. General, All-Purpose Test-Taking Skills

    A. Academic Preparation

        1. Test Content

        2. Test Format

        3. Planning for Tests

    B. Physical Preparation

    C. Improving Attitudes

    D. Reducing Anxiety

        1. Experience with Formats and Test-Taking Skills

        2. Self-Monitoring Attention

        3. Relaxation

    E. Improving Motivation

        1. External Motivation

        2. Internal Motivation

            a. Attributions

            b. Test-Taking attributions

II. Standardized Tests

    A. General Standardized Test Strategies

        1. Use of Separate Answer Sheets

        2. Elimination Strategies

        3. Guessing Strategies

        4. Using Time Wisely

    B. Specific Standardized Test Strategies

        1. Strategies for Reading Comprehension Subtests

        2. Strategies for Word Knowledge and Decoding Subtests

            a. Strategies for Vocabulary Subtests

            b. Strategies for Syllabication Subtests

            c. Strategies for Decoding Subtests

        3. Strategies for Math Computation Subtests

        4. Strategies for Math Concepts Subtests

        5. Strategies for Math Problem Solving Subtests

        6. Strategies for Science and Social Studies Subtests

III. Strategies for Classroom Tests

    A. Strategies for Objective Tests

    B. Strategies for Written Tests

        1. Strategies for Sentence Completion Items

        2. Strategies for Essay Tests

        3. Strategies for Performance Assessment.

## Pace

This outline of the test-taking skills curriculum is quite substantial. It may have you wondering how you can possibly fit it into what you have to teach in a school year!

    You can make this instruction most efficient by carefully integrating test-taking skills lessons into what you are teaching as part of the curriculum. For example, if students are studying information for which they are likely to be given an essay test, you might choose that time for teaching essay test-taking strategies. Similarly, if they are likely to be given multiple choice or other formats, they could spend time applying newly acquired information on these formats. In this way, you can integrate this training on taking tests into the time students spend studying the content (as shown in the essay test lesson example, below). It need take little additional instructional time.

You will probably have to allocate more time to lessons devoted to taking standardized tests. However, if your students have practiced test-taking skills throughout the year, the amount of time necessary for teaching these additional formats may be minimal. With careful planning, it should be possible to include the entire test-taking skills curriculum within one year of instruction, as an integrated part of learning the curriculum content, and have it impact positively on students' achievement during that year, as well as the years which follow.

# EXAMPLES

## Taking Essay Tests

We conclude by offering the reader illustrative examples on the teaching of sample test-taking skills using the instructional model described earlier in this chapter. First we present a sample lesson in which the "SNOW" strategy (Chapter 5) is taught. In this particular example, the strategy is being taught to a history class.

*Sample Lesson on Answering Essay Questions*
*Daily review.* Teacher: We have been practicing using test-taking skills for answering sentence completion ques-

tions. Jason, what is a sentence completion test item? [Jason responds] That's right, Jason, it's a sentence with a blank that you have to fill in. Now, let's go over the strategies for answering sentence completion. We all know what to do if you have read the question carefully and are sure you know the answer, don't we? What do you do, Christy? [C. responds]. That's right — write in the answer clearly and move on to the next question. But what are some things to do if you are not sure of the answer? What did we talk about last week, Jeff?....[Completes daily review].

**_Teacher presentation (and statement of objective)._** Today we are going to learn a strategy for answering essay questions. This time, I'm going to give you a special strategy to remember how to answer essay questions. Is everybody listening? The strategy is called **SNOW**. What's it called, everybody? Good, SNOW. You can remember that because you can use the SNOW strategy to SNOW, or impress, your teacher with your good answers on an essay test.

Now, SNOW is a first-letter strategy to help us remember the steps in this test-taking strategy. Each letter stands for an important step. [Shows on overhead projector].

The SNOW strategy for essay questions:

> **S** = **S**tudy the question;
>
> **N** = **N**ote important points;
>
> **O** = **O**rganize your thoughts;
>
> **W** = **W**rite to the point of the question.

_The first letter in **SNOW** is what, Ramon?_ [R. responds]. That's right, S. And as you can see, the S stands for _study_ the question. That means, make sure you know exactly what the question is asking before you go on. What's the next letter in SNOW, Marie? [M. answers]. That's right, N. And, see that the N stands for *note* the important points. That means, note down all the things you can think about that have to do with the question, and that you might put in your answer. What's the third letter, Bill? That's right, O. And the O stands for *organize* your thoughts before you write. That means, look at all the points you have written down, and see how they will fit together. The last letter in SNOW is W. And that letter stands for *write* directly to the point of the question. That means, write down your organized points to clearly and directly answer the question. Let's go over these points one more time .... [completes teacher presentation].

*Guided practice.* Now let's try some examples. [Shows overhead]. Look at this essay question:

ESSAY QUESTION:

1. Describe the causes of the War of 1812.

    Which do you think was the most important?

    Why?

Remember:

   **S**tudy the question,

   **N**ote down important points,

   **O**rganize your thoughts,

   **W**rite to the point of the question.

Now, using the SNOW strategy, what is the first thing we do, Leon? [ L. responds ]. Correct, Study the question. What does the question direct us to do, Sue? [S. responds]. First thing, describe the causes of the War of 1812. OK, we've been studying the War of 1812 in history, so we should know something about this. What does describe mean? Should we just list the causes that we can think of? [Class responds]. No, we should list the causes, but describe means we should write more about them than that. Is that all, Bill? [B. responds]. No, we must then say which cause we think is the most important. We must also say why we think so. So, let's highlight those [highlights on overhead] so we don't forget.

So, *describe* the causes, give the most important cause, and explain why. Did we study the question? [Class responds]. OK, let's go on. Note down important points. Well, what are they? What are the causes of the War of 1812? You tell me everything you can think of, and I'll write them down on the overhead. OK, Bill? [ B. answers, T. writes]: OK, Impressment of U.S. Sailors by the British. Anything else? Leon? [ L. responds ]. OK, British encouragement of Indian hostilities in the West. Anything else? [J. responds ]. OK, JoAnn, eagerness to annex Canada. Anything else?........[T. continues questioning].

OK, the next step is, *organize* the thoughts. What is the first thing we should write about, Sue? ... [T. continues questioning].

Now, the last thing is to *write* directly to the point of the question. Let's put this in sentence form together ... [T. continues soliciting responses].

***Independent practice.*** Now, I'm going to put another essay question on the overhead. This time, you go through all the steps of the SNOW strategy yourself. I'm going to give you 15 minutes to answer this one. Here it is [shows and reads overhead]:

ESSAY QUESTION

2.  Discuss the Battle of Lake Erie.

    Why was it an important battle in the War of 1812?

Remember:

> **S**tudy the question,
>
> **N**ote major points,
>
> **O**rganize your thoughts,
>
> **W**rite to the point of the question.

*Formative evaluation.* OK, time's up, pass in your papers, and we'll see how well you used your test-taking skills....

## Self-Monitoring Lesson

Here is an example of a lesson on reducing anxiety, using a self-monitoring strategy (from Chapter 3):

Self-Monitoring of Anxiety Lesson
*Daily review.* Over the last few days, we have been talking about how you can get yourself ready for tests. Are there any questions on what we've covered so far? No? OK, let's review what we discussed about how to prepare yourself physically. Joanna, what is one thing we talked about?......[T. continues review].

*Teacher presentation (and statement of objective).* Another way to do your best on tests is learn how to relax. If you can relax when you're taking a test, you can think more clearly, and you can earn a higher score than you can if you're tense and anxious. The problem is, sometimes we're tense and not relaxed, and we don't even know it. Do you think that ever happens to you, Susanne? [S. responds]. I bet it does. In fact, I'll bet that nearly everyone here sometimes gets tense and anxious and doesn't even know it. Marie, can you see how, if you're tense and nervous, you can't do as good a job on a test as you would if you were relaxed and confident? [M. responds]. Sure you can.

Well, the first thing you have to do to get yourself relaxed, is to figure out when you're getting tense. Today, we're going to learn how to use *self-monitoring* to keep ourselves relaxed when we're taking a test.

OK, Bill, how might you know that you're getting tense when you're taking a test? [B. responds]. That's one way — you could start biting your nails. What else could you do, anyone? (M. responds]. Good, you could tap your foot. Here are some other ways you can tell if you're getting nervous [shows overhead]:

THINGS WE DO WHEN WE'RE NERVOUS
1. Grinding or clenching teeth.
2. Tapping foot.
3. Rapid paced, shallow breathing.
4. Drumming fingers.
5. Clenched hands.
6. Tense muscles.
7. Rapid heart beat.
8. Tapping pencil.
9. Sweaty hands.
10. Fidgeting in seat.
11. Picking at face or hair.
12. Biting fingernails.
13. Giggling.

OK, let's go over these one at a time and discuss how each is a sign that you're nervous.....[T. continues discussion].

Now sometimes when you're taking a test, you're not anxious. Here are some things we do when we are relaxed [shows overhead]:

THINGS WE DO WHEN WE'RE RELAXED

1. Good, relaxed posture.

2. Relaxed muscle tone.

3. Slow, deep breathing.

4. Positive thoughts.

5. Calm physical manner, with no 'nervous' behaviors, such as fidgeting, biting fingernails, or pencil tapping.

6. Slow, relaxed heart beat.

OK, now let's go over each of these and talk about how you are relaxed when you are doing these things...[T. continues discussion].

*Guided practice.* I'm going to pass out a self-monitoring-sheet now, and we can go over it together, and talk about how you can measure whether you are tense or relaxed [T. passes out self-monitoring sheet]:

SELF-MONITORING SHEET
Relaxation

*Relaxed*: Good posture
Relaxed muscle tone.
Slow, deep breathing.
Positive thoughts.
Calm physical manner
Slow heart beat.

*Tense*: Grinding teeth.
Tapping foot, fidgeting.
Fast, shallow breathing.
Drumming fingers.
Clenched, sweaty hands.
Fast heart beat.

| Timer ring | Relaxed | Tense |
|------------|---------|-------|
| 1. | _____ | _____ |
| 2. | _____ | _____ |
| 3. | _____ | _____ |
| 4. | _____ | _____ |
| 5. | _____ | _____ |
| 6. | _____ | _____ |
| 7. | _____ | _____ |
| 8. | _____ | _____ |
| 9. | _____ | _____ |
| 10. | _____ | _____ |

*Independent practice.* Now, I have an assignment from our math class for you to work on. I want you to do your very best work on it. In addition, I want you to use your self-monitoring sheet. Every time the timer rings, I want you to think for a few seconds and decide whether you were tense or relaxed at the time the timer went off. Any questions? I'll pass out the work sheet and you can get started....

*Formative evaluation.* OK, time's up. Everybody pass in your worksheets and your self-monitoring sheets, and we'll see how well you did in math, and how well you did in monitoring your tension....

## Providing Feedback

We have mentioned the importance of formative evaluation in teaching any content or skill. Formative evaluation is necessary to determine whether the students are making adequate progress. However, in the case of test-taking skills, it may be difficult to determine solely on the basis of a tally of correct responses whether good test-taking skills had been employed. If there is reason for you to believe that a student may not be applying learned information efficiently on a test, it may be helpful to meet individually with the student to discuss the test. Using techniques similar to the interview techniques described in Chapter 2, you can get a better idea of what test-taking skills the student is or is not using.

For example, let us suppose that a student of yours received a lower grade on a test than you thought that student was likely to earn. A sample dialogue may be as follows:

### INTERVIEW ON TEST-TAKING SKILLS

Teacher: Steve, I would like to speak with you about this test. How do you think you did on it?

S:       OK, I guess.

T:       Well, I thought you could have done better on it, and I think we should talk about it. Is that all right with you?

S:       OK.

T:       Now, first, did you study for the test?

S:       Yes, I studied for two nights before the test. And I did my work in class.

T:       Did you eat well and get enough sleep before the test?

S:       Yes.

T:       Was there anything bothering you when you took the test?

S:      No.

T:      Well, let's look at some of the items that I thought
        you might have been able to answer correctly.
        Here's one [reads item]:

13. The Eskimos did not hunt:

      a. walrus

      b. seal

      c. crocodiles

      d. elk.

Why do you think you didn't answer this one correctly?

S:      I didn't remember what we read about Eskimos.

T:      So, why did you choose the answer you did?

S:      I didn't know what an elk was, so I guessed that
        one.

T:      But you do know where Eskimos live, don't
        you?

S:      Yes, in the cold countries.

T:      And you know something about animals, where
        they live, don't you?

S:      Yes.

T:      So, read these choices again and see if you see an
        animal that does not live in the cold country.

S:        Crocodile.

T:        That's right, so do you think crocodiles may be an animal that the Eskimos did not hunt?

S:        Yes.

T:        Well, see, you did know enough to answer that question — you just didn't think you did....

In the above example, the student's answers suggest he was reading the question carefully and reasoning through the answer using the partial knowledge he had. In other cases, teachers could determine whether students are reading the questions carefully, using answer sheets effectively, using time wisely, or doing any of the test-taking skills we have discussed in this book. Such interviews, based on actual test performance of students, can provide important information about the student's test-taking skills, and allow the teacher to help the student improve them. If there is not enough time to speak to students individually, it may be possible for the teacher to go through the test with the entire class, and suggest optimal ways for answering the questions. Nevertheless, some type of ongoing feedback can be very helpful in helping students do their best on tests.

## CONCLUSION

In this chapter, we have discussed effective teaching, the test-taking skills curriculum, and how these skills can be organized and taught in the classroom. We provided examples of lessons on test-taking skills that can be taught using effective teaching techniques. We hope you find these strategies and teaching techniques helpful, and that you use them frequently to help your students "show what they know!"

# Bibliography
# on Test Taking Skills

## Books

Browning, W.G. (1983). *Memory power for exams*. Lincoln, NE: Cliff's Notes. Describes study strategies, memory strategies, and test-taking skills.

Carman, R.A., & Adams, W.R. (1977). *Study skills: A student's guide for survival*. New York: Wiley. Describes a variety of study skills, and the 'SCORER' test-taking skill.

Erwin, B., & Dinwiddie, E.T. (1983). *Test without trauma*. New York: Grosset & Dunlap. Describes test anxiety and provides some strategies for dealing with it.

Hughes, C., Schumaker, J.B., & Deshler, D.D. (1987). *The test-taking strategy*. Lawrence, KS: EXCEL. Describes the Kansas University Institute for Research in Learning Disabilities strategy for test-taking skills.

Mastropieri, M.A., & Scruggs, T.E. (1987). *Effective instruction for special education*. Austin, TX: ProEd. Provides extensive information on the 'effective teaching' model, and provides a study and test-taking skills chapter.

Mastropieri, M.A., & Scruggs, T.E. (1991). *Teaching students ways to remember: Strategies for learning mnemonically*. Cambridge: Brookline Books. Provides a variety of memory-enhancing strategies that are useful in remembering academic content for tests.

Millman, J., & Pauk, W. (1969). *How to take tests*. New York: McGraw Hill. A very thorough book on the execution of test-taking skills. Directed more to the older, more independent student.

Phi Delta Kappa (Ed.) (1989). *Test anxiety*. Bloomington, IN: Phi Delta Kappa. An edited book of readings on the subject of test anxiety.

Sarason, I.G. (Ed.)(1980b). *Test anxiety: Theory, practice, and applications.* Hillsdale, NJ: Erlbaum. A scholarly, edited volume by one of the foremost authorities on test anxiety.

Schwarzer, R., van der Ploeg, H.M., & Spielberger, C.D. (1982). *Advances in test anxiety research* (Vol. 1). Hillsdale, NJ: Erlbaum. Edited volume of chapters describing original research on test anxiety.

Schwarzer, R., van der Ploeg, H.M., & Spielberger, C.D. (1983). *Advances in test anxiety research* (Vol. 2). Hillsdale, NJ: Erlbaum. Second volume of the series.

## Articles

Allen, G.J., Elias, M.J., & Zlotlow, S.F. (1980). Behavioral interventions for alleviative test anxiety: A methodological overview of current therapeutic practices. In I.G. Sarason (Ed.), *Test anxiety: Theory, research, and applications* (pp. 155-177). Hillsdale, NJ: Erlbaum.

Bangert-Drowns, R.L., Kulik, J.A., & Kulik, C. (1983). Effects of coaching programs on achievement test performance. *Review of Educational Research, 53,* 571-585.

Baron, J.B. (1990). Performance assessment: Blurring the edges among assessment, curriculum, and instruction. In A.B. Champagne, B.E. Lovitts, & B.J. Callinger (Eds.), *Assessment in the service of instruction* (pp. 127-148). Washington, DC: American Association for the Advancement of Science.

Callenbach, C.A. (1973). The effects of instruction and practice upon the standardized reading test scores of selected second grade students. *Journal of Educational Measurement, 10,* 25-30.

Costar, R. (1980). Scoring high in reading: The effectiveness of teaching achievement test-taking behaviors. *Elementary School Guidance and Counseling, 15,* 157-159.

Crehan, K.D., Gross, L.J., Koehler, R.A., & Slakter, M.J. (1978). Developmental aspects of test-wiseness. *Educational Research Quarterly, 3,* 40-44.

Denney, D.R. (1980). Self-control approaches to the treatment of anxiety. In I.G. Sarason (Ed.), *Test anxiety: Theory, research and applications* (pp. 209-244). Hillsdale, NJ: Erlbaum.

Diamond, J.J., Ayrer, J., Fishman, R., & Green, P. (1976). Are inner city children test-wise? *Journal of Educational Measurement, 14,* 39-45.

Diamond, J.J., & Evans, W. (1972). An investigation of the cognitive correlates of test-wiseness. *Journal of Educational Measurement, 14,* 39-45.

Dillard, M., Warrior-Benjamin, J., & Perrin, D.W. (1977). Efficacy of test-wiseness on test anxiety and reading achievement among black youth. *Psychological Reports, 41,* 1135-1140.

Dreisbach, M., & Keogh, B.K. (1982). Testwiseness as a factor in readiness test performance of young Mexican-American children. *Journal of Educational Psychology, 74,* 224-229.

Dunn, T.F., & Goldstein, L.G. (1959). Test difficulty, validity, and reliability as functions of selected multiple-choice item construction principles. *Educational and Psychological Measurement, 19,* 171-179.

Eakins, D.J., Green, D.S., & Bushnell, D. (1976). The effects of an instructional test-taking unit on achievement test scores. *Journal of Educational Research, 70,* 67-71.

Ford, V.A. (1973). *Everything you wanted to know about test-wiseness.* (ERIC Document Reproduction Service No. ED 093 912)

Fulk, B.J.M., & Mastropieri, M.A. (1990). Training positive attitudes. *Intervention in School and Clinic, 26,* 79-83.

Fulk, B.J.M., Mastropieri, M.A., & Scruggs, T.E. (1992). Mnemonic generalization training with learning disabled adolescents. *Learning Disabilities Research and Practice, 7,* 2-10

Fuyeo, V. (1977). Training test-taking skills: A critical analysis. *Psychology in the Schools, 14,* 180-184.

Gross, L.J. (1977). The effects of test-wiseness on standardized test performance. *Scandinavian Journal of Educational Research, 21*(2), 97-111.

Hughes, C. (1985). *A test-taking strategy for emotionally disturbed and learning disabled adolescents.* Unpublished doctoral dissertation, University of Florida, Gainesville.

Kalechstein, P., Kalechstein, M., & Doctor, R. (1981). The effects of instruction on test-taking skills in second grade black children. *Measurement and Evaluation in Guidance, 13,* 198-202.

Kreit, L.H. (1968). The effects of test-taking practice on pupil test performance. *American Educational Research Journal, 5,* 616-625.

Lee, P. & Alley, G.R. (1981). *Training junior high school LD students to use a test-taking strategy.* Lawrence, KS: Kansas University. (ERIC Document Reproduction Service No. ED 217 649).

Lepper, M.R., & Hodell, M. (1989). Intrinsic motivation in the classroom. In C. Ames & R. Ames (Eds.), *Research on motivation in education.* (pp. 73-106). New York: Academic Press.

Lifson, S., Scruggs, T. E., & Bennion, K. (1984). Passage independence in reading achievement tests: A follow-up. *Perceptual and Motor Skills, 58,* 945-946.

Lloyd, J., & Landrum, T. (1990). Self-recording of attending to task: Treatment components and generalization of effects. (pp. 235-632). In T.E. Scruggs & B.Y.L. Wong (Eds.), *Intervention research in learning disabilities*. New York: Springer Verlag.

McPhail, I.P. (1978). A psycholinguistic approach to training urban high school students in test-taking strategies. *The Journal of Negro Education, 47*, 168-176.

Meichenbaum, D., & Butler, L. (1980). Toward a conceptual model for the treatment of test anxiety: Implications for research and treatment. In I.G. Sarason (Ed.), *Test anxiety: Theory, research and applications* (pp. 187-208). Hillsdale, NJ: Erlbaum.

Metfessal, N.S., & Sax, G. (1958). Systematic biases in the keying of correct responses on certain standardized tests. *Educational and Psychological Measurement, 18*, 787-790.

Millman, J., Bishop, C.H., & Ebel, R. (1965). Analysis of test-wiseness. *Educational and Psychological Measurement, 25*, 707-726.

Oakland, T. (1972). The effects of test-wiseness materials on standardized test performance of pre-school disadvantaged children. *Journal of School Psychology, 10*, 355-360.

Ortar, G. (1960). Improving test validity by coaching. *Educational Research, 2*, 137-142.

Rowley, G.L. (1974). Which examinees are most favoured by the use of multiple choice tests? *Journal of Educational Measurement, 11*, 15-23.

Sarason, I.G. (1978). The Test Anxiety Scale: Concepts and research. In C.D. Spielberger & I.G. Sarason (Eds.). *Stress and anxiety* (Vol. 5). Washington, D.C.: Hemisphere.

Sarason, I.G. (1980a) Introduction to the study of test anxiety. In I.G. Sarason (Ed.), *Test anxiety: Theory, practice, and applications* (pp. 3-14). Hillsdale, NJ: Erlbaum.

Sarnacki, R.E. (1979). An examination of test-wiseness in the cognitive domain. *Review of Educational Research, 49,* 252-279.

Schunk, D.H. (1989). Self-efficacy and cognitive skill learning. In C. Ames & R. Ames (Eds.), *Research on motivation in education* (pp. 13-44). New York: Academic Press.

Scruggs, T.E. (1985). *The administration and interpretation of standardized achievement tests with learning disabled and behaviorally disordered elementary school children. Year Two Report.* Logan, UT: Utah State University, Developmental Center for Handicapped Persons. (ERIC Document Reproduction Service no. 260 560)

Scruggs, T. E., Bennion, K., & Lifson, S. (1985a). An analysis of children's strategy use on reading achievement tests. *Elementary School Journal, 85,* 479-484.

Scruggs, T. E., Bennion, K., & Lifson, S. (1985b). Learning disabled students' spontaneous use of test-taking skills on reading achievement tests. *Learning Disability Quarterly, 8,* 205-210.

Scruggs, T. E., & Lifson, S. A. (1985). Current conceptions of test-wiseness: Myths and realities. *School Psychology Review, 14,* 339-350.

Scruggs, T. E., & Lifson, S. A. (1986). Are learning disabled students 'test-wise'?: An inquiry into reading comprehension test items. *Educational and Psychological Measurement, 46,* 1075-1082.

Scruggs, T. E., & Marsing, L. (1988). Teaching test-taking skills to behaviorally disordered students. *Behavioral Disorders, 13,* 240-244.

Scruggs, T. E., & Mastropieri, M. A. (1986). Improving the test-taking skills of behaviorally disordered and learning disabled students. *Exceptional Children, 53,* 63-68.

Scruggs, T. E., & Mastropieri, M. A. (1988). Are learning disabled students "test-wise"?: A review of recent research. *Learning Disabilities Focus, 3*(2), 87-97.

Scruggs, T. E., Mastropieri, M. A., Tolfa, D., & Jenkins, V. (1985). Attitudes of behaviorally disordered students toward tests. Perceptual and Motor Skills, *60*, 467-470.

Scruggs, T. E., Mastropieri, M. A., & Veit, D. (1986). The effects of coaching on the standardized test performance of learning disabled and behaviorally disordered students. *Remedial and Special Education, 7*(5), 37-41.

Scruggs, T. E., & Tolfa, D. (1985). Improving the test-taking skills of learning disabled students. *Perceptual and Motor Skills, 60*, 847-850.

Scruggs, T. E., White, K., & Bennion, K., (1986). Teaching test-taking skills to elementary grade students: A meta-analysis. *Elementary School Journal, 87*, 69-82.

Slakter, M.J., Koehler, R.A., & Hampton, S.H. (1970). Learning test-wiseness by programmed texts. *Journal of Educational Measurement, 7*, 247-254.

Stevenson, P.C. (1976). Improving the learning disabled child's score on machine-scored tests. *Journal of Learning Disabilities, 9*, 17-19.

Taylor, C.F., & White, K.R. (1983). The effect of reinforcement and training on group standardized test behavior. *Journal of Educational Measurement, 19*, 199-209.

Tolfa, D., Scruggs, T. E., & Bennion, K. (1985). Format changes in reading achievement tests: Implications for learning-disabled students. *Psychology in the Schools, 22*, 387-391.

Tolfa, D., Scruggs, T. E., & Mastropieri, M. A. (1985). Attitudes of behaviorally disordered students toward tests: A replication. *Perceptual and Motor Skills, 61*, 963-966.

Veit, D. T., & Scruggs, T.E. (1986).  Can LD students effectively use separate answer sheets? *Perceptual and Motor Skills, 63,* 155-160.

Wahlstrom, M., & Boersma, F.J. (1968). The influence of test-wiseness upon achievement. *Educational and Psychological Measurement, 28,* 413-420.

Wine, J. (1971). Test anxiety and the direction of attention. *Psychological Bulletin, 76,* 92-104.

Wine, J. (1980). Cognitive-attentional theory of test anxiety.(pp. 349-385). In S.B.Sarason (Ed.), *Test anxiety: Theory, practice, and applications.* Hillsdale, NJ: Erlbaum.

# Test-Taking Skills Test Items

## Stem Options

1. The fragile plenophla plant:

    a. can grow in any soil;

    b. can withstand a wide variety of temperatures;

    c. tolerates poor moisture conditions;

    * d. grows best in very special soil.

2. The team sport of Botting is played:

    a. individually;

    * b. between two teams of five;

    c. by one player with a special bat;

    d. between two people.

3. The extinct Doplosaurus:

    a. walks upright;

    b. is a vegetarian;

    c. lives in the swamps;

    * d. had spikes on the end of its tail.

4. The tropical island of Tolua is known for:

    a. polar bears;

    * b. coconut trees;

    c. extensive glaciation;

    d. hosting the 1948 Winter Olympic Games.

5.  The Miniature Snell Hound was bred to:

    a. kill wolves;

    b. protect farm property;

    * c. enter the burrows of rodents and other small animals;

    d. herd cattle.

6.  The small village of Posey is known for:

    * a. its quiet lifestyle;

    b. traffic and pollution problems;

    c. population density;

    d. its strong industrial base.

## Similar Options

1.  The Cathra tree is found primarily in:

    a. arid climates;

    b. dry locations;

    c. barren soil;

    * d. rainy climates.

2.  The Western Redthroat:

    a. is a bird;

    * b. is a type of trout;

    c. has feathers and flies;

    d. builds nests and lays eggs.

3.  Shaving the head of the bride before marriage:

    * a. is a comical fable told to Balavian maidens;

b. is a Balavian tradition;

c. is a custom practiced in Balavia;

d. is a ritual seen in Balavia.

4. Manola refers to:

    a. Benalian currency.

    b. Money used in Benal.

* c. A popular dish in Benal.

    d. Coins from Benal.

5. The drug Apalopsis is now thought to be:

* a. a safe and effective medicine;

    b. hazardous to your health;

    c. harmful if taken internally;

    d. a damaging substance.

6. The climate of LaBruk is:

    a. damp;

* b. warm and sunny;

    c. dark and rainy;

    d. frequently moist.

## Absurd Options

1. Many reptiles are known to:

    a. migrate long distances;

    b. capture birds in flight;

    c. burrow in the snow when frightened;

* d. blend in with their surroundings.

2.  Twice yearly visits to the dentist are recommended:

    a. to keep your dentist wealthy;

    b. to keep your bills paid;

    c. to maintain a friendly relationship with your dentist;

    \* d. to prevent damage or disease in teeth and gums.

3.  The Civil War hero, Lester McKellips:

    a. shot down many enemy planes;

    \* b. led a successful charge against Confederate forces;

    c. captured many German soldiers;

    d. repelled a major tank offensive.

4.  The last space flight of astronaut John Moyers was:

    \* a. 1974;

    b. 1921;

    c. 1843;

    d. 1948.

5.  A product of the mineral slenite is commonly used for:

    a. increasing the numbers of mosquitos;

    b. weight gain for obese people;

    \* c. development of metal alloys;

    d. winning marathon races.

6.  One possible outcome of an atomic war is:

    a. an expanding economy;

b. an increase in maritime investment;

c. a population explosion;

\* d. a global warming trend.

## Specific Determiners

1. The element Gallicium:

    a. is never found in the Western Hemisphere;

    \* b. is often found in conjunction with Helatite;

    c. is found only in shale;

    d. is never mined outside of Honduras.

2. The poet Romantias:

    a. never revised his poems;

    \* b. was known for his poems about nature;

    c. always used the same meter;

    d. never travelled outside his home town.

3. In Northern Dugas:

    a. the climate is always the same;

    b. it is never sunny;

    c. it is always sunny;

    \* d. it often rains in the springtime.

4. Natives celebrating the Norien Festival:

    \* a. seldom invite outsiders to participate;

    b. always wear native clothing:

    c. never dance with the opposite sex;

    d. never sing after sundown;

5.   The early Renaissance painters:

   a. always used egg in their paint;

   b. never employed secular themes;

  * c. developed novel painting techniques;

   d. never accepted public donations.

6.   The actinotropic drugs:

   a. always cure infections;

  * b. are often used with older adults;

   c. are never associated with side effects;

   d. always act quickly.

# Index